The Civil War:
The South

Other Books in the History Firsthand Series:

The Civil War: The South

Thomas Streissguth, *Book Editor*

David L. Bender, *Publisher*
Bruno Leone, *Executive Editor*
Bonnie Szumski, *Editorial Director*
Stuart B. Miller, *Managing Editor*
David M. Haugen, *Series Editor*

Greenhaven Press, Inc., San Diego, California

Every effort has been made to trace the owners of copyrighted material. The articles in this volume may have been edited for content, length, and/or reading level. The titles have been changed to enhance the editorial purpose.

No part of this book may be reproduced or used in any form or by any means, electrical, mechanical, or otherwise, including, but not limited to, photocopy, recording, or any information storage and retrieval system, without prior permission from the publisher.

Library of Congress Cataloging-in-Publication Data

The Civil War: the South / Thomas Streissguth, book editor.
    p. cm. — (History firsthand)
    Includes bibliographical references (p.   ) and index.
    ISBN 0-7377-0408-X (pbk. : alk. paper) —
    ISBN 0-7377-0409-8 (lib. : alk. paper)
    1. Confederate States of America—History. 2. Confederate
States of America—Social conditions. 3. United States—History—
Civil War, 1861–1865—Social aspects. 4. United States—
History—Civil War, 1861–1865—Personal narratives, Confederate.
I. Streissguth, Thomas, 1958–   . II. Series.

E487 .C57   2001
973.7'13—dc21
                                        00-056047
                                             CIP

Cover photo: Digital Stock
Dover, 85
Library of Congress, 19, 32, 40, 98, 174, 184, 193, 215

Printed in the USA

Contents

Chapter 2: Early Victories

Chapter Preface

1. A Month with "The Rebels"
by Anonymous
Europeans took a great interest in the outcome of the
Civil War, which they believed had its counterpart in
the fight between republicans and monarchists on the
European continent. Early in the war, a British jour-
nalist recounts his experiences among the confident
civilians and soldiers of the Confederacy.

2. The Ride Around McClellan
by John Esten Cooke
Some of the most thrilling, and most dangerous, action of the Civil War occurred between opposing cavalry units. In the company of General James Ewell
Brown "Jeb" Stuart, a brilliant Confederate cavalry
commander, the author describes a dashing operation
around a befuddled Northern general.

3. Victory at Fredericksburg
by Robert Stiles
Inexperience and stubbornness contributed to tactical
blunders on both sides. At Fredericksburg, Virginia,
the South benefited from one of the worst such blunders committed by either side. A major of artillery
describes the bloody battle, in which thousands of
Northern soldiers died in an impossible charge up a
well-defended hill.

Chapter 3: Service in the Confederate Army

Chapter Preface

1. Cavalry Service
by William G. Stevenson
No matter what one's opinions of slavery or secession, living in the South meant fighting for the South.
A Northern sympathizer pressed into service in the
Confederate army stirs the reading public with his account of the desperate and deadly struggle.

Chapter 4: The War from Home

Chapter 5: Turning Points

out of formation and fighting on their own for survival. A New Yorker diligently serving in the Confederate army finds himself captured after the Battle of the Wilderness.

Chapter 6: The Death of the Confederacy

Foreword

In his preface to a book on the events leading to the Civil War, Stephen B. Oates, the historian and biographer of Abraham Lincoln, John Brown, and other noteworthy American historical figures, explained the difficulty of writing history in the traditional third-person voice of the biographer and historian. "The trouble, I realized, was the detached third-person voice," wrote Oates. "It seemed to wring all the life out of my characters and the antebellum era." Indeed, how can a historian, even one as prominent as Oates, compete with the eloquent voices of Daniel Webster, Abraham Lincoln, Harriet Beecher Stowe, Frederick Douglass, and Robert E. Lee?

Oates's comment notwithstanding, every student of history, professional and amateur alike, can name a score of excellent accounts written in the traditional third-person voice of the historian that bring to life an event or an era and the people who lived through it. In *Battle Cry of Freedom*, James M. McPherson vividly re-creates the American Civil War. Barbara Tuchman's *The Guns of August* captures in sharp detail the tensions in Europe that led to the outbreak of World War I. Taylor Branch's *Parting the Waters* provides a detailed and dramatic account of the American Civil Rights Movement. The study of history would be impossible without such guiding texts.

Nonetheless, Oates's comment makes a compelling point. Often the most convincing tellers of history are those who lived through the event, the eyewitnesses who recorded their firsthand experiences in autobiographies, speeches, memoirs, journals, and letters. The Greenhaven Press History Firsthand series presents history through the words of first-person narrators. Each text in this series captures a significant historical era or event—the American Civil War, the

Great Depression, the Holocaust, the Roaring Twenties, the 1960s, the Vietnam War. Readers will investigate these historical eras and events by examining primary-source documents, authored by chroniclers both famous and little known. The texts in the History Firsthand series comprise the celebrated and familiar words of the presidents, generals, and famous men and women of letters who recorded their impressions for posterity, as well as the statements of the ordinary people who struggled to understand the storm of events around them—the foot soldiers who fought the great battles and their loved ones back home, the men and women who waited on the breadlines, the college students who marched in protest.

The texts in this series are particularly suited to students beginning serious historical study. By examining these firsthand documents, novice historians can begin to form their own insights and conclusions about the historical era or event under investigation. To aid the student in that process, the texts in the History Firsthand series include introductions that provide an overview of the era or event, timelines, and annotated bibliographies that point the serious student toward key historical works for further study.

The study of history commences with an examination of words—the testimony of witnesses who lived through an era or event and left for future generations the task of making sense of their accounts. The Greenhaven Press History Firsthand series invites the beginner historian to commence the process of historical investigation by focusing on the words of those individuals who made history by living through it and recording their experiences firsthand.

Introduction

On March 6, 1857, Chief Justice Roger Brooke Taney of the Supreme Court delivered an opinion that, in the view of many, would decide the survival or the destruction of the United States. The bitter controversy over slavery that was dividing free states from slave states, North from South, was troubling the chief justice, a slave owner himself and a Democrat from the "border state" of Maryland. Although the verdict would settle one dispute between a slave and his master, Taney and the eight other members of the Supreme Court knew that it would do little to calm the controversy raging in the rest of the country. Not even the inaugural speech of the new Democratic president, James Buchanan, who had just appealed to "all good citizens" to accept the verdict no matter what it might be, would sway the opposite sides to agreement or compromise.

In the case of *Dred Scott v. Sandford,* the members of the Court, by a vote of seven to two, denied the appeal of Dred Scott, an elderly slave who had sued for his freedom on the grounds that he had lived for several years in Northern states where slavery was prohibited. In his opinion, Taney wrote that the authors of the Declaration of Independence and the Constitution did not extend the basic legal rights set out in these founding documents to black slaves. As mere property that could be bought and sold, slaves were naturally excluded from citizenship, from liberty, and from any participation in government.

To support the decision, Taney cited the Fifth Amendment to the Constitution, which provides that all citizens must be given due process of law before being deprived of their property. As a result, the U.S. Congress did not have the right to legislate against slavery and deprive slave owners of their property; therefore, all of the laws and compromises that restricted slavery in the new territories of the United States were unconstitutional. Slaves could not become citizens, could not vote, and could not sue in court. They would always be property, no matter where they traveled, and they could be transported freely by their owners throughout the country.

In a little more than four years the *Dred Scott* decision, authored and handed down by Taney, would help to ignite the Civil War, the deadliest and most destructive war in the nation's history. Yet Taney himself was no militaristic Southern firebrand calling for the dissolution of the Union. In 1828, with Andrew Jackson and Martin Van Buren, he had helped to establish the Democratic Party, which by the time of Buchanan's election was the largest political party in both the North and the South. As an opponent of the Bank of the United States and as a supporter of public authority over private enterprises, he had positioned himself as a champion of the rights of the common man against large business corporations and the federal government. Among the people of the South, and especially among Southern slave owners, he was favored as a reasonable, wise, and prudent jurist. But in the North, the *Dred Scott* decision transformed Taney into a hated representative of an immoral and backward institution whose opponents were readying to fight with arms as well as words.

A few days after the *Dred Scott* decision, Scott himself was freed by his owner, to live out the rest of his life as a laborer in St. Louis. In the meantime, the controversy over slavery burned even more fiercely. Southerners, and particularly Southern landowners who depended on slaves to raise their labor-intensive cash crops of cotton, rice, and tobacco, viewed the Northern abolition movement as a direct threat to their interests. They knew the end of slavery would mean an end to the agrarian economy that prevailed in the South, and they saw no reason to surrender their property or give up their way of life for the sake of Northern moralists and busybodies. They had always lived independently on self-sufficient estates where their word was law, and they would resist any tyrannical intrusion by the federal government on their rights since "states' rights" were guaranteed in various articles of the U.S. Constitution.

Lincoln Is Elected and the Confederacy Is Founded

The last straw for the Southern planter aristocracy was the election of Abraham Lincoln, which took place in November 1860. The platform of Lincoln's Republican Party stated that slavery should simply be restricted to states where it was already allowed and should not be extended to any new U.S. territories. Lincoln himself promised only to carry out this platform and vowed not to abolish slavery in states where it already existed. His views did not lessen the concerns of Southerners, however, who feared that if slavery were restricted in any way, the South would grow increasingly isolated. It would lose political influence in the U.S. Congress, and, little by little, Southerners would see their society torn apart by hundreds of new laws passed and judicial decisions taken under the influence of hostile Northern Republicans.

The defiant act of Southern secession began in South Carolina, where slavery had long made up a vital underpinning of the state's economy. On December 20, 1860, a convention of South Carolina politicians declared that the union between their state and the rest of the country was formally dissolved. On December 27 a South Carolina militia captured an isolated federal outpost known as Castle Pinckney, and the Palmetto flag of South Carolina was raised in place of the Stars and Stripes. Major Robert Anderson withdrew from the outpost, garrisoned his troops on a fortified island named Fort Sumter in the middle of Charleston harbor, and awaited orders.

Florida, Mississippi, Alabama, Georgia, Louisiana, and Texas followed South Carolina's lead and seceded by February 1, 1861. The state conventions that met to declare secession were attended by lawmakers and judicial officials who came overwhelmingly from among the planter aristocracy. They felt confident that they were following the best course of action for their states, for their families, and even for their slaves, who, in the natural order of things, were intended to work and live under the supervision and protection of the descendants of the European colonists. The Southern elites looked down on the manufacturing economy of the North and disdained Northern industrial cities, where foreign immigrants worked in unhealthy factories and where crime and immorality ran rampant. They also drew confidence from Southern cotton—"King Cotton" in Southern parlance—an economic lifeline that the North as well as Europe could never do without.

On February 8, 1861, at Montgomery, Alabama, the seceding states formed the Confederate States of America. Delegates adopted a constitution that specifically guaranteed the legality and perpetuation of slavery, and they elected Jefferson Davis as president and Alexander H. Stephens as vice president. In Washington, D.C., Secretary of War John Floyd, a Virginian with Southern sympathies, had 115,000 rifles taken from Northern arsenals and shipped to the South. The "lame duck" president Buchanan, a Democrat from Pennsylvania, agonized over the turn of events, avoided any military confrontation, and suggested that the Constitution somehow be revised to satisfy Northern as well as Southern interests. While he anxiously awaited the inauguration of his successor, Buchanan hoped that still-loyal Southern states, including Virginia and North Carolina, would remain within the Union and that the leaders of the Confederacy would fall into dissension, see the error of their ways, and renounce secession.

Lincoln was inaugurated on March 4, and early in the morning of April 12, Confederate shore batteries at Fort Johnson and four other locations opened fire on Major Anderson's garrison at Fort Sumter. Lincoln, the new president of a disunited nation, had ordered the garrison's resupply, knowing that federal ships would be unable to reach the fort under the guns of shore batteries. President Davis of the Confederate States of America had ordered the attack, knowing that Major Anderson was down to his last rations and was planning to surrender in a few days. "As the cannon spoke in Charleston," wrote Roger Butterfield in *The American Past*, "more than 40 years of compromises went up in smoke. . . . Already the Southern politicians were saying that the Confederacy would break up 'unless you sprinkle blood in the face of the people.' The South fired the first shot because the South felt the need for war."[1] On both sides, war seemed the only way to resolve the conflict over slavery, states' rights, and secession.

Anderson surrendered the fort after a thirty-four-hour bombardment. Realizing there was no alternative to armed force to reunite the country, Lincoln called for seventy-five-thousand volunteer troops, an action that prompted Virginia and then North Carolina to secede. Virginia's secession caused one of its citizens, Robert E. Lee, to resign his commission in the U.S. Army and join the newfounded Confederate army. Lee was followed by hundreds of his fellow Southern officers, among them the country's best military leaders: cavalry officer J.E.B. Stuart, Thomas "Stonewall" Jackson, and Nathan Bedford Forrest.

This mass defection of officers fueled war fever in the South, where men and women of all classes were drawing confidence from the belief that the Southerner's natural fighting ability—the enthusiasm for the duel and the affair of honor—would win the war. Not all Southern officers shared this enthusiasm and confidence, however. Sam Houston, who had fought for the independence of Texas and then served as governor and senator from that Southern state, warned, "Your fathers and husbands, your sons and brothers, will be herded at the point of the bayonet. You may, after the sacrifice of countless millions of treasure and hundreds of thousands of lives, win Southern independence. But I doubt it. I believe with you in the doctrine of States' Rights but the North is determined to preserve this Union."[2]

Houston was ignored by those who saw the advantages of the South's overall military strategy. The South may have had a smaller population, they explained, but it held the strategic advantage of interior lines of supply and communication; the Union armies must attack and conquer a vast, hostile territory that would be defended to the last by its inhabitants. In further support of their victory would be the 3 million slaves who provided the Confederacy with a labor supply that would free its soldier-farmers to leave their homes and fight indefinitely.

In May the Confederate government further expressed its confidence by moving its capital from Montgomery to Richmond, Virginia, home of the Tredegar Iron Works and other vital manufacturing operations. It was thought a Northern capital such as Richmond would help pull border states—Maryland, Kentucky, Delaware, and Missouri—into the Confederacy, or at least keep them neutral in the conflict. The new capital lay just one hundred miles from Washington, D.C.

There was one final aspect to the war that, to the people of the South, favored an ultimate Confederate victory. This was the self-interest of foreign nations, especially England and France. Once their manufacturing cities were starved of Southern cotton, these countries would suffer unemployment and social unrest that would threaten the survival of their governments. For the sake of self-preservation, they would ally themselves with the South and extend diplomatic recognition to its government. In the interest of keeping the peace at home, Southerners reasoned, these allies would provide ships, arms, and loans, and they would run any blockade that the Union could set in place along the Confederate coasts.

A Lack of Resources

Confederate confidence, however, could not replace the many vital resources that the South lacked. The Southern states had few factories, and most of them were concentrated in the states of Virginia, North Carolina, and Georgia. In Florida, whose long coastline might have provided an important export link with the outside world, there was only one operating factory during the Civil War. As a result, the South was forced to import many industrial goods, includ-

ing the rails and rolling stock of trains, which had been manufactured in Northern factories.

Even when well supplied, the most able of Confederate
officers were not quite prepared for the total war that ensued
after Fort Sumter. For the first time, submarines, machine
guns, chemical weapons, and railroads were used in war,
and the tactics changed along with the methods of killing.
Battlefield maneuvers no longer fit the Napoleonic mold,
which the officers had studied and prepared for their entire
careers; nor was the Civil War a hit-and-run guerrilla operation such as the recent Mexican War, experienced by
Robert E. Lee and many others. The magnitude of the war—
the fact that it involved a total effort by both the military and
civilians—took both sides somewhat by surprise, with the
North being better able to adjust and adapt to the situation.

Nevertheless, the Civil War began with Southern victories. The first major battle, known as First Manassas, or Bull
Run, took place in July 1861 after a Union offensive into
northern Virginia. After a day of smoke and confusion on
the battlefield, the Confederate army held the field. For
months afterward, while Lincoln called for more volunteer
regiments from the Northern states, Union officers fortified
their positions around Washington, dreading a Confederate
attack on the capital.

But the attack never came. Fortified by the victory at Bull
Run, Southern military and political leaders decided to hold
their ground and wait for the collapse that would result from
panic and dissension in the North. By the middle of February 1862, Ulysses S. Grant had led a Union army into Forts
Henry and Donelson in western Tennessee, keys to the central states of the Confederacy. At the Battle of Shiloh in
April 1862, the Confederates were stopped by the Union
army along the Tennessee-Mississippi border. Later that
month, the port of New Orleans, the principal exporting
point for Southern cotton, fell to a Union naval force under
Admiral David Farragut.

In the East the Confederate army scored a series of important victories. In May the Confederate general Joseph

Confederate general Robert E. Lee is cheered on by his troops after his victory at the Battle of Chancellorsville. Through bold maneuvers Lee's 60,000-man army soundly defeated General Joseph Hooker's troops, which numbered 130,000.

Johnston blocked a sweep through the peninsulas of southeastern Virginia by Union armies under General George McClellan. Meanwhile, Stonewall Jackson pinned down four federal armies in the Shenandoah Valley of Virginia, preventing them from aiding McClellan in the peninsula. Robert E. Lee, who had replaced the wounded Johnston after Seven Pines, defeated the Union army with Jackson's help at Second Manassas on August 29 and 30, 1862. Lee followed up the victory with an invasion of Maryland, which began on September 5. Lee hoped to threaten Washington from the west and force the federal government to ask for terms and recognize the Confederacy. But McClellan fought Lee and Jackson to a stalemate at Sharpsburg, Maryland, on September 17. Also known as Antietam, this battle eventually pushed Lee back across the Potomac River into Virginia.

The success of General Grant's campaign in Tennessee, and the failure of a Confederate offensive in Kentucky, also helped to keep the important border states out of the Confederate camp. Missouri, Maryland, Delaware, and Kentucky stayed in the Union, keeping the majority of their able-bodied soldiers for Union service and preventing their manufacturing industries from resupplying Southern armies. In addition, the people of mountainous eastern Tennessee and western North Carolina stayed loyal to the Union, and a large portion of western Virginia split off and declared itself a loyal new state: West Virginia.

Dissension at Home

Although they had joined the Confederacy with enthusiasm, the governors of the South were not united in their effort to support the cause with troops. State militias were held back for home defense and were not sent to the war front; if they were sent, it was with the agreement that service must be of limited duration. Governor Joseph Brown of Georgia commissioned ten thousand second lieutenants in his own state's militia in order to keep them out of the reach of Confederate recruiters. Other governors insisted that defense of their home states overrode any need for a national army to defend cities and farms in other sections of the South. Underlying these policies was the principle of states' rights, which the South had declared as the crucial reason for the Civil War in the first place. For governors and state legislators, states' rights held not only for laws and government but also for the produce of farms and factories. The state of North Carolina declared that all shoes, uniforms, and other equipment produced within its borders were to be furnished only to North

Carolina troops. In 1864 the state of Virginia demanded, and won, control over the largest factory within its borders and priority on the use of trains passing through the state.

Another problem for the South was taxation, a practice also resisted on the principles of limited government and states' rights. Desperate for money to buy military supplies, the Confederate government passed an income tax law on April 24, 1863, which taxed income at a rate as high as 15 percent, taxed farm profits, and imposed a levy of one-tenth of all food produced on Southern farms. For Southern farmers and small landholders, this last "tax in kind" quickly became a hated institution. The tax was collected by agents who worked the farms nearest railroads for convenience and diverted many of the goods collected into their own private accounts.

Taxes alone did not fuel the disillusionment and dissension that grew within the South almost from the start of the war. The demands of a war economy brought about shortages in clothing, food, construction materials, tools, and many other essential goods that had to be imported through a tight Union naval blockade. In the meantime, within the ranks of the Confederate army, the fighting spirit faded quickly as sickness, boredom, fatigue, and danger took their toll. Lacking new volunteers, the Confederate congress passed the first national conscription act on April 16, 1862, just one year after the attack on Fort Sumter and one year before the North passed its own conscription law. All able-bodied white men between eighteen and thirty-five were subject to three years' service (the age limit was raised to forty-five on September 27, 1862). Exemptions were granted for those who had important duties as farm overseers, factory managers, and government administrators. Because each state governor had the right to request whatever exemptions he pleased, and because the majority of exemptions were granted to members of the upper and middle classes, resentment among workers and farm laborers, who actually did the fighting, grew. At the same time, the conscription effort fragmented as General Braxton Bragg was allowed to set up his own conscription service for Alabama, Mississippi, and Tennessee.

The duplication of the conscription effort, food levies, and harsh policies led to further confusion and resistance on the part of the Southern public. In *The Oxford History of the American People,* historian Samuel Eliot Morrison writes:

> War was the Confederacy's only business. Fighting for independence and race supremacy, the Southerners gave their government more, and asked less, than did the Northern people. Yet the latest generation of Southern historians has proved that selfishness, indifference, and defeatism played a great part in losing the "lost cause." And there was a shrewd instinct on the part of poor whites that it was "a rich man's war and a poor man's fight."[3]

By late 1863 the Confederate economy was failing. Military supplies were not getting to the fronts in Virginia and elsewhere, and volunteers were becoming scarce. Confederate armies that did manage to remain in the field were running out of ammunition. At home, the population suffered hunger, fear, and discontent that frayed their loyalty to the Confederacy. Southern morale took a severe blow with the death of Stonewall Jackson after the Battle of Chancellorsville in early May 1863. Another turning point was the Union victory at Vicksburg, Mississippi, in July 1863. During a six-week siege of the city, the citizens of Vicksburg had lived in increasingly desperate conditions, their supplies of food cut off and their homes subject to bombardment. As Edwin C. Bearss writes in *The Civil War Battlefield Guide,* all of the effort and suffering was in vain:

> The Vicksburg campaign and siege was a milestone on the road that led to the final success of the Union army and the reunification of the nation. . . . The Confederacy was now divided. In the weeks between March 29 and July 4, Grant had destroyed a Confederate army of 40,000 at a cost of 10,000 battle casualties. He had captured 260 cannon, 60,000 stand-of-arms, and more than two million rounds of ammunition. The Confederacy could not afford such a loss of men and materiel.[4]

In addition to winning control of the Mississippi River, the fight for Vicksburg made clear to the people of the South

that the war would not be confined to the front lines in remote mountains and battlefields. This was a total war,
fought against civilians as well as soldiers, in which the purpose was to starve and beat an entire population into sub-
mission. If there was any hope that the Union intended to
score a purely military victory, it vanished by the time of
Union general William Sherman's destruction of Atlanta,
Georgia, and his "march to the sea" in which Union troops
laid waste a one-hundred-mile swath of small towns and fertile farmland between Atlanta and Savannah, Georgia.

The Collapse of the Confederacy

A slow but steady economic collapse took hold after the important Union victories at Vicksburg and at Gettysburg,
Pennsylvania. Strapped for money and unable to secure loans
from abroad, the Confederate government could pay only
ridiculously low prices for food, creating ever-worsening
poverty for Southern farmers. Men who left their farms to
fight left overburdened families to carry out the demanding
chores of raising crops as best they could. Essential farm
equipment broke down and could not be repaired. At the
same time, many cotton and tobacco farmers would not give
up their cash crops to plant badly needed food, thus starving
the army further. Speculators hoarded dry goods as well as
food and cash crops, holding their supplies out of the market
until the prices rose and they could sell them again for a
steep profit. The lack of supplies and the shortage of labor
also slowed the work of essential factories. Bankrupt operations were nationalized (placed under the control of the national government), an action that led to increasing waste and
inefficiency. Nationalization created further dissent among
state officials. In North Carolina, textile milling became a
state-owned operation, carried out under the orders of Governor Zebulon Vance to avoid nationalization of the industry
by the Confederate government.

For the duration of the war, Confederate money and state
money, as well as bonds, circulated throughout the South,
creating confusion and further weakening the cause. Many

merchants and farmers preferred state money to the national currency, and by the end of the war, Confederate national currency would be of legendary worthlessness. Inflation remained high, despite an attempt to bolster Confederate money by taking one-third of all banknotes out of circulation in February 1864.

The loss of the Mississippi valley in the summer of 1863 had cut the South in two, preventing the Confederate army from reinforcing itself with troops from the west. At the end of 1863, a Union army under Grant secured the important supply and transportation center at Chattanooga, Tennessee, a victory that allowed General Sherman a base from which to launch his attack on Atlanta. In July, General Lee's ambitious invasion of the North had been stopped at Gettysburg, and now Lee was forced into a long retreat through Virginia in order to prevent an all-out Union attack on Richmond.

These setbacks further weakened the Confederate cause in Europe, where President Lincoln's Emancipation Proclamation had turned public opinion against the policy of aiding the South. Worse, the threat of a cotton shortage, which Southern planters had so confidently relied on early in the war, was having little effect, especially in Britain. British cotton dealers found themselves profiting from the steep rise in cotton prices caused by the war in the United States, and they took the opportunity to sell off surplus stocks they had been holding in their warehouses. English linen and flax mills ran at capacity to make up the shortages, and the British merchant marine enjoyed a sharp dropoff in competition from the United States, where military action and blockades claimed the use of freighters as well as military vessels. British arms merchants did a brisk business in sales of powder, rifles, ammunition, and other war goods; they had no interest in seeing the South victorious or even in seeing the Civil War come to an end.

While Southern men had gone to the front, and as the Union armies swept through Tennessee, Georgia, and Virginia, the Southern slaves grew rebellious. In *American Slavery, 1619–1877*, Peter Kolchin describes their tactics:

Slaves took advantage of their masters' absence at war to drag
their feet, chip away at rules and regulations, and break down traditional discipline. . . . Wherever Union troops approached, the
transformation of master-slave relations became unmistakeable as
slaves sensed their impending liberation. They became unruly and
"demoralized"; they defiantly refused to obey orders and talked
back to masters; and they ran away, at first one by one, and then
in droves.[5]

At the same time, hostility grew between landowning
planters and ordinary farmers, who resentfully saw their
own men fighting and dying for the Southern aristocracy.
Nonslaveholders who lived in the deep woods and mountainous regions of the South, a population that expressed little support for secession in the first place, resisted conscription and in some cases aided the Union armies passing
near their homes.

By 1864 a shortage of labor made planting and harvest-
ing nearly impossible in several regions, and many Southern fields were left fallow or unharvested. The Union blockade prevented the Confederacy from exporting its cotton and
importing arms and ammunition from Europe. Southern
families experienced shortages of flour, sugar, and coffee,
which was replaced by ground parched corn and other un-
savory concoctions. Medical supplies, salt to preserve meat,
and cattle hides to make shoes and belts also grew scarce.
Even goods that could be harvested or produced often could
not be packaged and distributed because of packaging material shortages, including paper, wood, burlap, and twine.

With no replacement locomotives, parts, or rails—and no
native supply of iron to cast wheels, boilers, and spare
parts—the Southern rail system gradually broke down. Local and private interest again played a role, as the patchwork
network of private rail companies passed up army supply in
favor of more lucrative contracts transporting civilian goods.
The system grew increasingly congested as the Union
armies seized vital rail centers, including Vicksburg, Chattanooga, and finally Atlanta. By the end of 1864 the South
was broken into isolated regions, and even mules and wag-

ons, the most basic items of military transport, were growing scarce.

In an attempt to lessen the shortages, the Confederate army carried out impressment (seizure) of food and livestock. The impressed goods were supposed to be paid for, but the system was exploited by corrupt officers and caused growing public resentment and evasion of the law. Meanwhile, at the front, desertion from the army increased as soldiers, seeing the futility of the Confederate cause, returned to their homes to protect their families from the bandits and marauders who were infesting the countryside. Ambushes and assassinations of Confederate officers and government officials began occurring. Entire counties in Virginia, South Carolina, and Mississippi went over to the cause of war resisters and submitted to the rule of organized bands of deserters.

Surrender

In November 1864 Abraham Lincoln was reelected president, promising to carry the war out to total victory, and the Confederacy's last hope of reaching a settlement with the North and of preserving its independence abruptly ended. In February 1865 the Confederate congress took a last desperate step by allowing slaves to be armed and enrolled in the military ranks. The act did not grant freedom for service, however, and only a few black troops were mustered into the Confederate army, too late to have any effect on the war's outcome.

In April 1865 the Union armies captured Petersburg, a rail center lying just south of Richmond. With only 25,000 troops under his command, Lee desperately maneuvered to the west to join up with a Confederate force in North Carolina. But the trap closed around the Army of Northern Virginia, and on April 9 Lee surrendered to Grant at Appomattox Courthouse, Virginia. On April 26, Johnston surrendered to Sherman at Raleigh, North Carolina. More than 250,000 Southern troops had been killed in a failing cause, and the only hope for an easy restoration and reconstruction of the South also died with President Lincoln, who was assassinated in Washington on April 14.

The South would take decades to recover from the destruction and humiliation of its defeat in the Civil War. The war ruined Southern industry and transportation, and the Union armies had left entire cities in smoldering ruins. Although most soldiers went home to rebuild their homes and farms, many Southerners fled west to escape the expected Northern tyranny. The long and contentious political reconstruction of the South and the bitter debates over laws governing the freed black slaves would form the legacy of the pride, confidence, and secession fever that had gripped the people of the South in the years prior to the Civil War.

Notes

1. Roger Butterfield, *The American Past: A History of the United States from Concord to Hiroshima, 1775–1945.* New York: Simon and Schuster, 1947, pp. 164–65.

2. Quoted in James P. Reger, *Life in the South During the Civil War.* San Diego: Lucent Books, 1997, p. 73.

3. Samuel Eliot Morrison, *The Oxford History of the American People.* New York: Oxford University Press, 1965, p. 667.

4. Edwin C. Bearss, *The Civil War Battlefield Guide.* Boston: Houghton Mifflin, 1990, pp. 134–35.

5. Peter Kolchin, *American Slavery, 1619–1877.* New York: Hill and Wang, 1993, pp. 204–205.

Chapter 1

Secession and First Fights

Chapter Preface

For many Southerners, the secession of South Carolina from the United States on December 20, 1860, represented the beginning of the end: a final, long-sought resolution to the bitter political fight with the North over slavery and states' rights. Within weeks, the landowners who made up a majority of legislators in the Southern states were taking their cue from the leading men of South Carolina and declaring their own states free and independent members of the Confederate States of America. Finally, the people of the South were free to live, conduct business, and make laws as they saw fit, and the South became the equal of the North—perhaps even the greater power. An agricultural economy that provided the world with its most essential goods, the sheer size of the new country (as large as western continental Europe), the fighting abilities of Southern men, and the corruption of the North would, Southerners believed, provide their section with all the advantages if it should ever come to war. The colonists' fight against England, in which outnumbered ragtag militias defeated the greatest military power on Earth, provided the South with an inspiring example of a successful bid for freedom.

In their early enthusiasm and confidence, however, the people of the South made miscalculations. Support for secession was not unanimous, even in the original seven seceding states and even less so in the border states. And the necessities of war had changed since the Napoleonic wars, the last great military conflict of the nineteenth century. Industry, finance, communications, and transportation now played the key roles, overriding bravery, discipline, and national spirit. Yet if the leaders of the Confederacy played their economic and military cards well, the fight could be carried on and won, and the Confederate States of America could succeed as an independent nation.

Imbecility, Buffoonery, and Vulgar Malignity

John M. Daniel

For Southern patriots, the election of Abraham Lincoln proved the final straw in the bitter and worsening rivalry with the North. Lincoln's avowed policy of limiting the spread of slavery posed a direct challenge to Southern economic interests. Southern politicians and editorialists nearly unanimously agreed that the new president would personally see to the South's subjugation, by blocking southern-favored legislation in Congress, by appointing abolitionist judges to the courts, and by imposing military occupation on recalcitrant Southern states. Those who favored secession found their most prominent target yet in the president-elect, who personified the abolitionist sentiment that was rapidly pushing the country toward war.

On the occasion of Lincoln's inauguration, on March 4, 1861, John M. Daniel of the Richmond *Examiner* welcomed the nation's new leader with a viciously eloquent and sarcastic literary portrait. Likening the Kentucky-born country lawyer to a bumptious western barkeep was just the beginning for Daniel who, by his final sentence, had turned Lincoln into a bloodthirsty tyrant with no regard for the threatened republic or for its Constitution.

This Fourth of March, the memorable day of a memorable year, will not attain a less celebrity in future history than the Roman Ides of the same month [on the ides of March,

Excerpted from *The "Richmond Examiner" During the War; or The Writings of John M. Daniel*, by John M. Daniel (New York: n.p., 1868).

44 B.C., Julius Caesar was assassinated, marking the end of the Roman republic]. We stand to-day between two worlds. Here a past ends, here a future begins. The Republic of the United States on this day bids farewell to the style, the policy, the principles that have borne it in the lifetime of a man from insignificance to grandeur. . . . To-day we take leave of our policy and our practice, of the manners and of the men who have marked and guided the career that is ended. The line of those high personages, who will hereafter be known in history, only, as the Presidents, ends to-day; and that generation who shall learn their lives and their character from the pages of the future [historian Edward] Gibbon who will narrate the decline and fall of the United States will compare them with the despicable tyrants whose dismal roll commences on the peristyle of the Capitol under the light of the sun now shining, as the youth of our day contrast the grand succession of Roman Consuls with the Divine Tiberius, with the Neros, with the Claudes, the Caligulas who defiled their seats and prostituted their titles, when another such day of March had separated another constitutional republic from another disguised despotism.

President Buchanan is the last of the family of Presidents. He was learned in their school, looked and spoke, and endeavored to act and think as they did. The historical character which he desired to leave was one like theirs, and, whatever the failure in essentials, the style and outward mould was that of the Madisons, the Monroes, the Van Burens, Tylers, Polks. We would be uncandid to say that he has filled their measure; for though the retiring President is one of the most distinguished figures of our day; has passed a long life in the most splendid employment; and though he must always be reckoned as one of the most eminent and celebrated statesmen of this country, it is impossible to deny that his administration has been unequal to his fame; that he has left chaos where he found order, ruin where he found prosperity; or that much of this disaster may be fairly charged to his faults of character and policy.

It is difficult to say which was the most unfortunate, his

foreign or his domestic system. It is certain that the former was the least American ever followed by a Democratic President. Even Mr. Buchanan himself would probably admit that his domestic policy has not been successful. Yet few who have either spirit, intelligence, or national pride, can fail to regret the retiring President while gazing on his successor. Whatever his particular faults, in person he well represented the decency, the dignity, the decorum of the country.

The Faults of Mr. Lincoln

To replace him in the White House, Northern Federalism has sent a creature whom no one can hear with patience or look on without disgust. We have all heard of a King of Shreds and Patches; but in the first of "Free Presidents" we have the delightful combination of a western county lawyer

The election of Abraham Lincoln to the Presidency of the United States sparked great Southern discontent and has been considered as one reason for the Confederate states' secession from the union.

with a Yankee barkeeper. No American of any section has read the oratory with which he has strewn his devious road to Washington, condensed lumps of imbecility, buffoonery, and vulgar malignity, without a blush of shame. It is with a bitter pang that we remember that these samples of utter blackguardism have already gone to all the earth translated into all the languages that men speak, to justify the worst representations that our worst enemies have ever made of the national degradation to which they pretend republican government must ever lead.

But all personal antipathies are lost in the deep sentiment of apprehension which must affect every thinking man when he remembers the terrible significance of this beastly figure. Whether we are to be governed by a gentleman or ruled by a baboon, would matter comparatively little were each the representative of constitutional government. But with Lincoln comes something worse than slang, rowdyism, brutality, and all moral filth; something worse than all the tag and rag of Western grog-shops [taverns] and Yankee factories. . . . With all that comes arbitrary power. With all those comes the daring and reckless leader of Abolitionists, who has long proclaimed and now is effecting his purpose of destroying every federative feature of the constitution, all the peculiar characteristics of the separate State systems, to consolidate them all by mere numerical force in one grand anti-slavery community.

The new President has climbed to his place on the fragments of a shattered Confederacy [referring to the entire nation bound under the Articles of Confederation], and the mere necessity of things will force him to deluge them in blood long before the Ides of another March has come again. A citizen of this State [the United States], returning to his country after an absence of years, and alighting at daybreak in the streets of its Capital, heard the bugle's reveille, the roll of drums and the tramp of armed guards there till he fancied himself back in Venice, or arriving in Warsaw. The first of the Free Presidents gets to the seat of government in the disguise of a foreigner and by the nocturnal flight of a conscience-stricken murderer in purpose; he is inaugurated to-day as John Brown was hung, under the mouths of cannon leveled at the citizens whom he swears to protect; and with the bayonets of mercenary battalions commanding every road to the fountain of mercy and justice. What can come of all this but civil war and public ruin?

Jefferson Davis to the Confederate Congress

Jefferson Davis

A passionate defender of slavery, Jefferson Davis was also an experienced military man, having graduated from West Point in 1828 and served with distinction in the Mexican War of 1846–48. As secretary of war under President Franklin Pierce during the mid-1850s, he proposed the capture and annexation of Cuba to the United States as an additional slave state. After the secession of his home state, Mississippi, Davis resigned his seat in the U.S. Senate. He won election as president of the newly founded Confederate States of America in February 1861.

Although the people of the South were firmly behind secession, Davis knew he had to make his case to the rest of the world and to history. In this crucial speech to the Confederate Congress, delivered on April 29, 1861, Davis recounts the many burdens placed on the Southern states by the North, defends slavery, describes the general good health and well-being of Africans brought to North America for their labor, and criticizes the deceitful actions of the Northern government in its deliberate provocation of war in early April 1861.

Gentlemen of the Congress: It is my pleasing duty to announce to you that the Constitution framed for the establishment of a permanent Government for the Confederate States has been ratified by conventions in each of those States to which it was referred. To inaugurate the Govern-

Reprinted from Jefferson Davis's address to the Confederate Congress, Montgomery, Alabama, April 29, 1861.

ment in its full proportions and upon its own substantial basis of the popular will, it only remains that elections should be held for the designation of the officers to administer it. There is every reason to believe that at no distant day other States, identified in political principles and community of interests with those which you represent, will join this Confederacy, giving to its typical constellation increased splendor, to its Government of free, equal, and sovereign States a wider sphere of usefulness, and to the friends of constitutional liberty a greater security for its harmonious and perpetual existence. It was not, however, for the purpose of making this announcement that I have deemed it my duty to convoke you at an earlier day than that fixed by yourselves for your meeting. The declaration of war made against this Confederacy by Abraham Lincoln, the President of the United States, in his proclamation issued on the 15th day of the present month, rendered it necessary, in my judgment, that you should convene at the earliest practicable moment to devise the measures necessary for the defense of the country. The occasion is indeed an extraordinary one. It justifies me in a brief review of the relations heretofore existing between us and the States which now unite in warfare against us and in a succinct statement of the events which have resulted in this warfare, to the end that mankind may pass intelligent and impartial judgment on its motives and objects. During the war waged against Great Britain by her colonies on this continent a common danger impelled them to a close alliance and to the formation of a Confederation, by the terms of which the colonies, styling themselves States, entered "*severally* into a firm league of friendship with each other for their common defense, the security of their liberties, and their mutual and general welfare, binding themselves to assist each other against all force offered to or attacks made upon them, or any of them, on account of religion, sovereignty, trade, or any other pretense whatever." In order to guard against any misconstruction of their compact, the several States made explicit declaration in a distinct article— that "*each* State *retains its* sovereignty, freedom, and independence, and every power, jurisdiction, and right which is not by this Confederation *expressly delegated* to the United States in Congress assembled.". . . .

Majority Rules

The people of the Southern States, whose almost exclusive occupation was agriculture, early perceived a tendency in the Northern States to render the common government subservient to their own purposes by imposing burdens on commerce as a protection to their manufacturing and shipping interests. Long and angry controversies grew out of these attempts, often successful, to benefit one section of the country at the expense of the other. And the danger of disruption arising from this cause was enhanced by the fact that the Northern population was increasing, by immigration and other causes, in a greater ratio than the population of the South. By degrees, as the Northern States gained preponderance in the National Congress, self-interest taught their people to yield ready assent to any plausible advocacy of their right as a majority to govern the minority without control. They learned to listen with impatience to the suggestion of any constitutional impediment to the exercise of their will, and so utterly have the principles of the Constitution been corrupted in the Northern mind that, in the inaugural address delivered by President Lincoln in March last, he asserts as an axiom, which he plainly deems to be undeniable, that the theory of the Constitution requires that in all cases the majority shall govern; and in another memorable instance the same Chief Magistrate did not hesitate to liken the relations between a State and the United States to those which exist between a county and the State in which it is situated and by which it was created. This is the lamentable and fundamental error on which rests the policy that has culminated in his declaration of war against these Confederate States. . . .

When the several States delegated certain powers to the United States Congress, a large portion of the laboring population consisted of African slaves imported into the colonies by the mother country. In twelve out of the thirteen

States negro slavery existed, and the right of property in slaves was protected by law. . . .

The climate and soil of the Northern States soon proved unpropitious to the continuance of slave labor, whilst the converse was the case at the South. Under the unrestricted free intercourse between the two sections, the Northern States consulted their own interests by selling their slaves to the South and prohibiting slavery within their limits. The South were willing purchasers of a property suitable to their wants, and paid the price of the acquisition without harboring a suspicion that their quiet possession was to be disturbed by those who were inhibited not only by want of constitutional authority, but by good faith as vendors, from disquieting a title emanating from themselves. As soon, however, as the Northern States that prohibited African slavery within their limits had reached a number sufficient to give their representation a controlling voice in the Congress, a persistent and organized system of hostile measures against the rights of the owners of slaves in the Southern States was inaugurated and gradually extended. . . .

In the meantime, under the mild and genial climate of the Southern States and the increasing care and attention for the well-being and comfort of the laboring class, dictated alike by interest and humanity, the African slaves had augmented in number from about 600,000, at the date of the adoption of the constitutional compact, to upward of 4,000,000. In moral and social condition they had been elevated from brutal savages into docile, intelligent, and civilized agricultural laborers, and supplied not only with bodily comforts but with careful religious instruction. Under the supervision of a superior race their labor had been so directed as not only to allow a gradual and marked amelioration of their own condition, but to convert hundreds of thousands of square miles of the wilderness into cultivated lands covered with a prosperous people; towns and cities had sprung into existence, and had rapidly increased in wealth and population under the social system of the South; the white population of the Southern slaveholding States had augmented from about 1,250,000 at the date of the adoption of the Constitution to more than 8,500,000 in 1860; and the productions of the South in cotton, rice, sugar, and tobacco, for the full development and continuance of which the labor of African slaves was and is indispensable, had swollen to an amount which formed nearly three-fourths of the exports of the whole United States and had become absolutely necessary to the wants of civilized man. With interests of such overwhelming magnitude imperiled, the people of the Southern States were driven by the conduct of the North to the adoption of some course of action to avert the danger with which they were openly menaced. . . .

Fort Sumter: Unprovoked Aggression

Early in April [1861] the attention of the whole country, as well as that of our commissioners [diplomats in Washington], was attracted to extraordinary preparations for an extensive military and naval expedition in New York and other Northern ports. These preparations commenced in secrecy, for an expedition whose destination was concealed, only became known when nearly completed, and on the 5th, 6th, and 7th of April transports and vessels of war with troops, munitions, and military supplies sailed from Northern ports bound southward. Alarmed by so extraordinary a demonstration, the commissioners requested the delivery of an answer to their official communication of the 12th of March, and thereupon received on the 8th of April a reply, dated on the 15th of the previous month, from which it appears that during the whole interval, whilst the commissioners were receiving assurances calculated to inspire hope of the success of their mission, the Secretary of State and the President of the United States had already determined to hold no intercourse with them whatever; to refuse even to listen to any proposals they had to make, and had profited by the delay created by their own assurances in order to prepare secretly the means for effective hostile operations. That these assurances were given has been virtually confessed by the Government of the United States by its sending a messenger to Charleston to give notice of its purpose to use force if opposed in its intention of supplying Fort Sumter. No more striking proof of the absence of good faith in the conduct of the Government of the United States toward this Confederacy can be required than is contained in the circumstances which accompanied this notice. According to

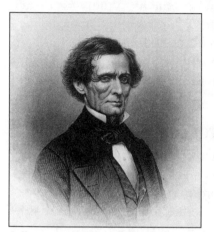

the usual course of navigation the vessels composing the expedition designed for the relief of Fort Sumter might be expected to reach Charleston Harbor on the 9th of April. Yet, with our commissioners actually in Washington, detained under assurances that notice should be given of any military movement, the notice was not addressed to *them*, but a messenger was sent to Charleston to give the notice to the Governor of

Jefferson Davis felt that because of the actions of the U.S. government, the South's secession was justified.

South Carolina, and the notice was so given at a late hour on the 8th of April, the eve of the very day on which the fleet might be expected to arrive.

That this maneuver failed in its purpose was not the fault of those who contrived it. A heavy tempest delayed the arrival of the expedition and gave time to the commander of our forces at Charleston to ask and receive the instructions of this Government. Even then, under all the provocation incident to the contemptuous refusal to listen to our commissioners, and the tortuous course of the Government of the United States, I was sincerely anxious to avoid the effusion of blood, and directed a proposal to be made to the commander of Fort Sumter, who had avowed himself to be nearly out of provisions, that we would abstain from directing our fire on Fort Sumter if he would promise not to open fire on our forces unless first attacked. This proposal was refused and the conclusion was reached that the design of the United States was to place the besieging force at Charleston between the simultaneous fire of the fleet and the fort. There remained, therefore, no alternative but to direct that the fort should at once be reduced. This order was executed by General Beauregard with the skill and success which were naturally to be expected from the well-known character of that gallant officer; and although the bombardment lasted but thirty-three hours our flag did not wave over its battered walls until after the appearance of the hostile fleet off Charleston. Fortunately, not a life was lost on our side, and we were gratified in being spared the necessity of useless effusion of blood, by the prudent caution of the officers who commanded the fleet in abstaining from the evidently futile effort to enter the harbor for the relief of Major Anderson [commander of the fort]. . . .

A Declaration of War

Not only does every event connected with the siege reflect the highest honor on South Carolina, but the forbearance of her people and of this Government from making any harsh use of a victory obtained under circumstances of such peculiar provocation attest to the fullest extent the absence of any purpose beyond securing their own tranquillity and the sincere desire to avoid the calamities of war. Scarcely had the President of the United States received intelligence of the failure of the scheme which he had devised for the reënforcement of Fort Sumter, when he issued the declaration of war against this Confederacy which has prompted me to convoke you. In this extraordinary production that high functionary affects total ignorance of the existence of an independent Government, which, possessing the entire and enthusiastic devotion of its people, is exercising its functions without question over seven sovereign States, over more than 5,000,000 of people, and over a territory whose area exceeds half a million of square miles. He terms sovereign States "combinations too powerful to be suppressed by the ordinary course of judicial proceedings or by the powers vested in the marshals by law." He calls for an army of 75,000 men to act as a *posse comitatus* ["county force"] in aid of the process of the courts of justice in States where no courts exist whose mandates and decrees are not cheerfully obeyed and respected by a willing people. He avows that "the *first* service to be assigned to the forces called out" will be not to execute the process of courts, but to capture forts and strongholds situated within the admitted limits of this Confederacy and garrisoned by its troops; and declares that "this effort" is intended "to maintain the perpetuity of popular government." He concludes by commanding "the persons composing the combinations aforesaid"—to wit, the 5,000,000 of inhabitants of these States—"to retire peaceably to their respective abodes within twenty days." Apparently contradictory as are the terms of this singular document, one point is unmistakably evident. The President of the United States called for an army of 75,000 men, whose *first* service was to be to capture our forts. It was a plain declaration of war which I was not at liberty to disregard because of my knowledge that under the Constitution of the United States the President was usurping a power granted exclusively to the Congress. He is the sole organ of communication between that country and foreign powers. The law of nations did not permit me to question the authority of the Executive of a foreign nation to declare war against this Confederacy. Although I might have refrained from taking active measures for our defense, if the States of the Union had all imitated the action of Virginia, North Carolina, Arkansas, Kentucky, Tennessee, and Missouri, by denouncing the call for troops as an unconstitutional usurpation of power to which they refused to respond, I was not at liberty to disregard the fact that many of the States seemed quite content to submit to the exercise of the power assumed by the President of the United States, and were actively engaged in levying troops to be used for the purpose indicated in the proclamation. Deprived of the aid of Congress at the moment, I was under the necessity of confining my action to a call on the States for volunteers for the common defense, in accordance with the authority you had confided to me before your adjournment. I deemed it proper, further, to issue proclamation inviting application from persons disposed to aid our defense in private armed vessels on the high seas, to the end that preparations might be made for the immediate issue of letters of marque and reprisal

Jefferson Davis: Virtues and Faults

The Confederate defeat resulted from many factors, but for many observers the most tempting target for blame has been the man who led its government. In The Cause Lost, *historian William C. Davis, who has written several important books on the Civil War and the Confederacy, carries out a brief psychoanalysis of Jefferson Davis, finding him to be, after all is said and done, a rather ordinary man.*

The litany of shortcomings that associates and observers found and still find in Davis is a long one, though it is all too often forgotten that each has a positive obverse. Yes, he was obstinate, but he was also determined. He was oversensitive to criticism, yet able to cope with mind-numbing pressures. His indecisiveness went hand in hand with a commendable reluctance to be hasty. Certainly he was hot-tempered and impulsive, but he was also impervious to fear. He demonstrated a consistently poor judgment of character but was also trusting to a fault. Very susceptible to sycophants, he nevertheless stimulated genuine love and admiration in those who knew him intimately. Obsessed with detail, he also possessed a phenomenal grasp of legal and military minutiae, and to his equal obsession with always being right must be matched the diligent effort he made in forming conclusions that to his mind were right. In all of these pairings, the former are not traits to make a man endearing. But that does not mean that there is anything either unusual or mysterious about them.

William C. Davis, *The Cause Lost: Myths and Realities of the Confederacy.* Lawrence: University Press of Kansas, 1996.

which you alone, under the Constitution, have power to grant. I entertain no doubt you will concur with me in the opinion that in the absence of a fleet of public vessels it will be eminently expedient to supply their place by private armed vessels, so happily styled by the publicists of the United States "the militia of the sea," and so often and justly relied on by them as an efficient and admirable instrument of defensive warfare. I earnestly recommend the immediate passage of a law authorizing me to accept the numerous proposals already received. I cannot close this review of the acts of the Government of the United States without referring to a proclamation issued by their President, under date of the 19th instant, in which, after declaring that an insurrection has broken out in this Confederacy against the Government of the United States, he announces a blockade of all the ports of these States, and threatens to punish as pirates all persons who shall molest any vessel of the United States under letters of marque issued by this Government. Notwithstanding the authenticity of this proclamation you will concur with me that it is hard to believe it could have emanated from a President of the United States. Its announcement of a mere paper blockade is so manifestly a violation of the law of nations that it would seem incredible that it could have been issued by authority; but conceding this to be the case so far as the Executive is concerned, it will be difficult to satisfy the people of these States that their late confederates will sanction its declarations—will determine to ignore the usages of civilized nations, and will inaugurate a war of extermination on both sides by treating as pirates open enemies acting under the authority of commissions issued by an organized government. If such proclamation was issued, it could only have been published under the sudden influence of passion, and we may rest assured mankind will be spared the horrors of the conflict it seems to invite. . . .

"Our Cause Is Just and Holy"

In conclusion, I congratulate you on the fact that in every portion of our country there has been exhibited the most patriotic devotion to our common cause. Transportation companies have freely tendered the use of their lines for troops and supplies. The presidents of the railroads of the Confederacy, in company with others who control lines of communication with States that we hope soon to greet as sisters, assembled in convention in this city, and not only reduced largely the rates heretofore demanded for mail service and conveyance of troops and munitions, but voluntarily proffered to receive their compensation, at these reduced rates, in the bonds of the Confederacy, for the purpose of leaving all the resources of the Government at its disposal for the common defense. Requisitions for troops have been met with such alacrity that the numbers tendering their services have in every instance greatly exceeded the demand. Men of the highest official and social position are serving as volunteers in the ranks. The gravity of age and the zeal of youth rival each other in the desire to be foremost for the public defense; and though at no other point than the one heretofore noticed have they been stimulated by the excitement incident to actual engagement and the hope of distinction for individual achievement, they have borne what for new troops is the most severe ordeal—patient toil and constant vigil, and all the exposure and discomfort of active service, with a resolution and fortitude such as to command approbation and justify the highest expectation of their conduct when active valor shall be required in place of steady endurance. A people thus united and resolved cannot shrink from any sacrifice which they may be called on to make, nor can there be a reasonable doubt of their final success, however long and severe may be the test of their determination to maintain their birthright of freedom and equality as a trust which it is their first duty to transmit undiminished to their posterity. A bounteous Providence cheers us with the promise of abundant crops. The fields of grain which will within a few weeks be ready for the sickle give assurance of the amplest supply of food for man; whilst the corn, cotton, and other staple productions of our soil afford abundant proof that up to this period the season has been propitious.

We feel that our cause is just and holy; we protest solemnly in the face of mankind that we desire peace at any sacrifice save that of honor and independence; we seek no conquest, no aggrandizement, no concession of any kind from the States with which we were lately confederated; all we ask is to be let alone; that those who never held power over us shall not now attempt our subjugation by arms. This we will, this we must, resist to the direst extremity. The moment that this pretension is abandoned the sword will drop from our grasp, and we shall be ready to enter into treaties of amity and commerce that cannot but be mutually beneficial. So long as this pretension is maintained, with a firm reliance on that Divine Power which covers with its protection the just cause, we will continue to struggle for our inherent right to freedom, independence, and self-government.

Why Did That Green Goose Anderson Go into Fort Sumter?

Mary Boykin Chesnut

> A member of a leading Charleston family, Mrs. James Ches-
> nut lived at the summit of the Southern landowning aristoc-
> racy. In the autumn of 1860, her father-in-law became the
> first Southern politician to resign from the U.S. Senate; at the
> start of the war her husband was serving as an aide to General
> Beauregard, who gave the order to fire on Fort Sumter. She
> was well acquainted with South Carolina politicians, judges,
> governors, and businessmen, and after the war began she took
> great interest in the Confederacy's military tactics, hearing
> much of it firsthand from the generals and civilian leaders
> who put that strategy in place.
>
> Through it all, Mary Boykin Chesnut faithfully kept a diary
> which has become one of the best-known eyewitness docu-
> ments to the Southern experience of the Civil War. In April
> 1861, she watched with growing excitement and fear the bom-
> bardment of Fort Sumter in Charleston harbor, knowing that it
> would lead to war and, most probably, the death of loved ones
> and an end to her comfortable and happy way of life.

We came home, and soon Mr. Robert Gourdin and Mr. Miles called. Governor Manning walked in, bowed gravely, seated himself by me, and said, in mock heroic style and with a grand wave of his hand: "Madame, your country

Reprinted from an April 1861 entry from Mary Boykin Chesnut's diary as it appears in *A Diary from Dixie*, edited by Ben Ames Williams (Boston: Houghton Mifflin, 1949).

is invaded." When I had breath to speak, I asked: "What does he mean?" "He means this. There are six men-of-war outside the Bar [Charleston Harbor]. Talbot and Chew have come to say that hostilities are to begin. [South Carolina] Governor [Francis W.] Pickens and [General P.T.] Beauregard are holding a Council of War." Mr. Chesnut then came in. He confirmed the story. [Confederate congressman Louis T.] Wigfall next entered in boisterous spirits. He said "there was a sound of revelry by night . . ."

In any stir or confusion my heart is apt to beat so painfully. Now the agony was so stifling that I could hardly see or hear. The men went off almost immediately, and I crept silently to my room where I sat down to a good cry.

Mrs. Wigfall came in and we had it out, on the subject of civil war. We solaced ourselves with dwelling on all its known horrors, and then we added some remarks about what we had a right to expect with Yankees in front and Negroes in the rear. "The slave owners must expect a servile insurrection, of course," said Mrs. Wigfall, to make sure that we were unhappy enough.

Suddenly loud shouting was heard. We ran out. Cannon after cannon roared. We met Mrs. Allan Green in the passageway with blanched cheeks and streaming eyes. Governor Means rushed out of his room in his dressing gown and begged us to be calm. "Governor Pickens has ordered, in the plenitude of his wisdom, seven cannon to be fired as a signal to the 7th Regiment. [Northern commander at Fort Sumter, Major Robert] Anderson will hear, as well as the 7th Regiment. Now you go back and be quiet. Fighting in the streets has not begun yet." So we retired. Dr. Gibbes calls Mrs. Green, Dame Placid. There was no placidity today, no sleep for anybody last night. The streets were alive with soldiers and other men shouting, marching, singing. Wigfall, the "stormy petrel," was in his glory, the only thoroughly happy person I saw. Today things seem to have settled down a little. One can but hope. Lincoln or [Secretary of State] Seward have made such silly advances, and then far sillier drawings back. There may be a chance for peace after all.

Demanding a Surrender

Things are happening so fast. My husband has been made an aide-de-camp of General Beauregard. Three hours ago we were quietly packing to go home. The Convention had adjourned. Now he tells me the attack upon Fort Sumter may begin tonight.

It depends upon Anderson and the fleet outside. John Manning came in with his sword and red sash, pleased as a boy to be on Beauregard's staff while the row goes on. He has gone with Wigfall to Captain Hartstein with instructions.

Mrs. Hayne [wife of South Carolina senator Robert Hayne] called. She had, she said, but one feeling; pity for those who are not here.

Jack Preston, Willie Allston—"the take-life-easy," as they are called—with John Green, "the big brave," have gone down to the Island and volunteered as privates. Seven hundred men were sent over. Ammunition wagons rumbling along the streets all night. Anderson burning blue lights; signs and signals for the fleet outside, I suppose.

Today at dinner there was no allusion to things as they stand in Charleston Harbor, but there was an undercurrent of intense excitement. There could not have been a more brilliant circle. In addition to our usual quartette (Judge Withers, Langdon Cheves and Trescot), our two Ex-Governors dined with us; Means and Manning. These men all talked so delightfully, and for once in my life I listened.

That over, business began in earnest. Governor Means had found a sword and a red sash and brought them for Colonel Chesnut, who has gone to demand the surrender of Fort Sumter.

And now, patience! We must wait. Why did that green goose Anderson go into Fort Sumter? Then everything began to go wrong. Now they have intercepted a letter from him urging them to let him surrender. He paints the horrors likely to ensue if they will not. He ought to have thought of all that before he put his head in the hole.

APRIL 12th.—Anderson will not capitulate!

Yesterday was the merriest, maddest dinner we have had yet. Men were more audaciously wise and witty. We had an unspoken foreboding it was to be our last pleasant meeting. Mr. Miles dined with us today. Mrs. Henry King rushed in. "The news? I come for the latest news! All of the men of the King family are on the Island," of which fact she seemed proud.

While she was here, our peace negotiator or our envoy came in; that is, Mr. Chesnut returned. His interview with Colonel [actually Major] Anderson had been deeply interesting but he was not inclined to be communicative, and wanted his dinner. He felt for Anderson. He had telegraphed to President Davis for instructions as to what answer to give Anderson. He has now gone back to Fort Sumter with additional instructions. When they were about to leave the wharf, A.H. Boykin sprang into the boat in great excitement. He thought himself ill used; a likelihood of fighting and he to be left behind.

I do not pretend to go to sleep. How can I? If Anderson does not accept terms at four o'clock, the orders are he shall be fired upon.

I count four by St. Michael's chimes, and I begin to hope. At half past four, the heavy booming of a cannon! I sprang out of bed and on my knees, prostrate, I prayed as I never prayed before.

There was a sound of stir all over the house, a pattering of feet in the corridor. All seemed hurrying one way. I put on my double-gown and a shawl and went to the house top. The shells were bursting. In the dark I heard a man say: "Waste of ammunition!" I knew my husband was rowing about in a boat somewhere in that dark bay, and that the shells were roofing it over, bursting toward the Fort. If Anderson was obstinate, Mr. Chesnut was to order the Forts on our side to open fire. Certainly fire had begun. The regular roar of the cannon, there it was! And who could tell what each volley accomplished of death and destruction.

The women were wild, there on the house top. Prayers from the women and imprecations from the men; and then a shell would light up the scene. Tonight, they say, the forces are to attempt to land. The *Harriet Lane* had her wheel house smashed and put back to sea.

We watched up there, and everybody wondered why Fort Sumter did not fire a shot. Today Miles and Manning, Colonels now, and aides to Beauregard, dined with us. The latter hoped I would keep the peace. I gave him only good words, for he was to be under fire all day and night, in the bay carrying orders.

Last night—or this morning, truly—up on the house top, I was so weak and weary I sat down on something that looked like a black stool. "Get up, you foolish woman! Your dress is on fire," cried a man; and he put me out. It was a chimney, and the sparks caught my clothes; but my fire had been extinguished before it broke out into a regular blaze.

Do you know, after all that noise, and our tears and prayers, nobody has been hurt. Sound and fury signifying nothing! A delusion and a snare!

The First Day of the War

Louisa Hamilton comes here now. This is a sort of news center. Jack Hamilton, her handsome young husband, has all the credit of a famous battery which is made of railroad iron. Mr. Petigru calls it The Boomerang, because it throws the balls back the way they came. So Louisa Hamilton tells us. She had no children during her first marriage; hence the value of this lately achieved baby. To divert Louisa from the glories of "the Battery" of which she raves, we asked if the baby could talk yet. "No, not exactly, but he imitates the big gun. When he hears that, he claps his hands and cries 'Boom Boom.'" Her mind is distinctly occupied by three things; Lent Hamilton, whom she calls "Randolph," the baby, and the big gun—and it refuses to hold more.

[Outspoken secessionist Roger] Pryor of Virginia spoke from the piazza of the Charleston Hotel. I asked what he said. Louisa, the irreverent woman, replied: "Oh, they all say the same thing, but he made great play with that long hair of his, which he is always tossing aside."

Somebody came in just now and reported Colonel Chesnut asleep on the sofa in General Beauregard's room. After two such nights he must be so tired as to be able to sleep anywhere.

Just bade farewell to Langdon Cheves. He is forced to go home, to leave this interesting place. He says he feels like the man who was not killed at [the ancient Battle of] Thermopylae. I think he said that that unfortunate had to hang himself when he got home for very shame; maybe fell on his sword, which was a strictly classic way of ending matters.

I do not wonder at Louisa Hamilton's baby. We hear nothing, can listen to nothing. Boom Boom goes the cannon all the time. The nervous strain is awful, alone in this darkened room.

"Richmond and Washington Ablaze," say the papers. Blazing with excitement! Why not? To us these last days' events seem frightfully great. We were all, on that iron balcony, women. Men we only see now at a distance. Stark Means marching under the piazza at the head of his regiment held his cap in his hand all the time he was in sight. Mrs. Means was leaning over, looking with tearful eyes. "Why did he take his hat off?" said an unknown creature. Mrs. Means stood straight up. "He did that in honor of his mother. He saw me." She is a proud mother, and at the same time most unhappy. Her lovely daughter Emma is dying before her eyes of consumption. At that moment, I am sure Mrs. Means had a spasm of the heart. At least she looked as I sometimes feel. She took my arm and we came in.

Biding Time

APRIL 13th.—Nobody hurt, after all. How gay we were last night. Reaction after the dread of all the slaughter we thought those dreadful cannons were making such a noise in doing. Not even a battery the worse for wear.

Fort Sumter has been on fire. He has not yet silenced any of our guns, or so the aides—still with swords and red sashes by way of uniform—tell us. But the sound of those guns makes regular meals impossible. None of us go to table, but tea trays pervade the corridors going everywhere. Some of the anxious hearts lie on their beds and moan in solitary misery. Mrs. Wigfall and I solace ourselves with tea in my room. These women have all a satisfying faith. "God is on our side," they cry. When we are shut in, we, Mrs. Wigfall and I, ask: "Why?" Answer: "Of course, He hates the Yankees! You'll think that well of Him."

Not by one word or look can we detect any change in the demeanor of these Negro servants. Lawrence sits at our door, as sleepy and as respectful and as profoundly indifferent. So are they all. They carry it too far. You could not tell that they even hear the awful noise that is going on in the bay, though it is dinning in their ears night and day. And people talk before them as if they were chairs and tables, and they make no sign. Are they stolidly stupid, or wiser than we are, silent and strong, biding their time.

So tea and toast come. Also came Colonel Manning, A.D.C., red sash and sword, to announce that he had been under fire—and didn't mind! He said gayly: "It is one of those things! A fellow never knows how he will come out of it until he is tried. Now I know I am a worthy descendant of my old Irish hero of an ancestor, who held the British officer before him as a shield in the Revolution and backed out of danger gracefully!" We talked of St. Valentine's Eve, of the Maid of Perth, and the drop of the white doe's blood that sometimes spoiled all.

The war steamers are still there outside of the Bar. And there were people who thought the Charleston Bar "no good" to Charleston. The Bar is our silent partner—a sleeping partner—yet in this fray it is doing us yeoman service.

Surrender

APRIL 15th.—I did not know that one could live such days of excitement. They called: "Come out! There is a crowd coming." A mob, indeed; but it was headed by Colonels Chesnut and Manning. The crowd was shouting and showing these two as messengers of good news whom they were escorting to Beauregard's Headquarters. Fort Sumter had surrendered! Those up on the house top shouted to us: "The Fort is on fire." That had been the story once or twice before.

When we had calmed down, Colonel Chesnut, who had taken it all quietly enough, if anything more unruffled than usual in his serenity, told us how the surrender came about.

Wigfall was with them on Morris Island when he saw the fire in the Fort, jumped in a little boat, and with his handkerchief as a white flag, rowed over to Fort Sumter. Wigfall went in through a porthole [and helped arrange the surrender of the Fort]. When Colonel Chesnut arrived shortly after, and was received by the regular entrance, Colonel Anderson told him he had need to pick his way warily, for it was all mined. As far as I can make out, the Fort surrendered to Wigfall. But it is all confusion. Our flag is flying there. Fire engines have been sent to put out the fire. Everybody tells you half of something and then rushes off to tell someone else, or to hear the last news.

In the afternoon Mrs. Preston, Mrs. Joe Heyward and I drove around the Battery. We were in an open carriage. What a changed scene! The very liveliest crowd I think I ever saw. Everybody talking at once, all glasses still turned on the grim old Fort.

[William] Russell, the English reporter for the Times, was there. They took him everywhere. One man studied up his [British novelist William Makepeace] Thackeray to converse with him on equal terms. Poor Russell was awfully bored, they say. He only wanted to see the Forts and get news that was suitable to make an interesting article. Thackeray was stale news over the water.

Mrs. Frank Hampton and I went to see the camp of the Richland troops. South Carolina College had volunteered to a boy. Professor Venable (The Mathematical) intends to raise a company from among them for the war, a permanent company. This is a grand frolic, no more—for the students at least!

Even the staid and severe-of-aspect Clingman is here. He says Virginia and North Carolina are arming to come to our rescue; for now the United States will swoop down on us. Of that we may be sure. We have burned our ships. We are obliged to go on now.

Losing an Opportunity at Bull Run

Edward Porter Alexander

On July 21, 1861, the Confederate and Union armies met for the first time at Manassas, Virginia, about twenty-five miles from Washington, D.C. Expecting a grand spectacle and a smashing defeat of the Confederates, the people of Washington turned out in force to witness this Battle of Bull Run from nearby hilltops. Unfortunately, after a confused melee lasting several hours, the Union forces were in headlong retreat back to the Potomac, sharing the roads with companies of panicked civilians now in fear for their lives.

Also onhand to witness the Confederate victory was Jefferson Davis and his leading generals, including Joseph Johnston, P.T. Beauregard, and Stonewall Jackson. As General E.P. Alexander recounts, these gentlemen committed a serious blunder in not following up their opportunity to pursue the Union army to the streets of the capital itself. Instead, they hesitated, not sure of how and where to undertake the pursuit, mistrustful of reports they received of the enemy's confusion, and confident that the victory would soon be followed by more victories and ultimately an easy defeat of the enemy. Instead of a decisive victory, however, the Battle of Bull Run turned out to be a missed opportunity—the first, and last, such opportunity ever presented to the leaders of the Confederacy.

After two o'clock the roar of the battle began to increase again, and about three, a new battery opened fire from

Excerpted from *Military Memoirs of a Confederate*, by E.P. Alexander (New York: Scribner's, 1907).

a point farther to my left than any previous firing. It was plainly engaged in enfilading one of the opposing lines, and I watched anxiously to see which. Presently one of its shells burst high in the air over the Federal position. I was satisfied that I could be of no further service at the signal station, and I rode for the field. Had I not seen the direction in which that new battery was firing I would soon have believed our army to have been already defeated from the swarms of stragglers met upon my road. A few had flesh wounds, and all had stories of disaster which had left few survivors of their commands. President Davis had arrived at Manassas from Richmond, early in the afternoon, and, even then, stragglers from the field had met the train at the Junction, a half-mile from the station, with such alarming stories that the conductor feared to carry the train farther. After persuasion, however, he sent the President and an aide up to the station on a locomotive.

At the station horses and a guide were procured, and Mr. Davis rode to the field. He soon encountered the procession of stragglers and heard their stories. He was so impressed by their numbers that he said to an officer riding with him, "Fields are not won where men desert their colors as ours are doing."

A Great Opportunity

Quite near the field, the road crossed a small stream. Here the surgeons had established field hospitals, and about these and under shade of the trees the crowd of wounded, attendants, and stragglers was extensive. As he had ridden along the road, the President had frequently called upon men to turn back to the field, and some had done so. Here he seemed to fear that the whole army was in retreat. As he rode his horse into the stream he drew his rein, and with a pale, stern face, and in a loud, ringing voice he shouted, "*I am President Davis. Follow me back to the field!*" Not far off, Stonewall Jackson, who had been shot through the hand, but had disregarded it until victory was assured, was now having his hand dressed by Surgeon Hunter McGuire. Jackson did not catch the President's words, and McGuire repeated them to him. Jackson quickly shouted: "We have whipped them! They ran like sheep! Give me 5000 fresh men, and I will be in Washington City to-morrow morning." In that sentence, as we shall see, appears almost the only evidence of appreciation among our leaders, on that field, of the great opportunity now before them.

The enemy were routed. Jackson saw their demoralization, and felt that, if rapidly followed up, it would spread and might involve the capital itself. And every soldier should have seen in it at least a good chance to cut off and capture many thousands of fugitives retreating by long and roundabout roads.

There was little effort, worthy of the name, even to do this. Our small bodies of cavalry did their best and captured about as many prisoners as they could handle. In all 871 unwounded were taken. But to fully improve such an opportunity much more was necessary. All the troops best situated to cut the line of retreat should have been put in motion. Not only staff-officers, but generals themselves, should have followed up to inspire and urge pursuit. The motto of our army here would seem to have been, "Build a bridge of gold for a flying enemy."

Jackson's offer to take Washington City the next morning with 5000 men had been made to the President as he arrived upon the field, probably about five o'clock. It was not sunset until 7:15, and there was a nearly full moon. But the President himself and both generals spent these precious hours in riding over the field where the conflict had taken place. Doubtless it was an interesting study, the dead and badly wounded of both sides being mostly where they had fallen, but it was not war to pause at that moment to consider it. One of the generals—Beauregard, for instance— should have crossed Bull Run at Ball's Ford or Stone Bridge with all the troops in that vicinity, and should have pushed the pursuit all night. Johnston should have galloped rapidly back to Mitchell's Ford and have marched thence on Centreville with Bonham, Longstreet, and Jones, who had not been engaged. No hard fighting would have been needed. A threat upon either flank would doubtless have been sufficient; and, when once a retreat from Centreville was started, even blank volleys fired behind it would have soon converted it into a panic.

It would be vain to speculate how far the pursuit might have been pushed or what it might have accomplished had all the available force been energetically used. We were deficient in organization, discipline, and transportation, but these deficiencies are no sufficient excuse for not attempting the game of war. In that game, to use the slang of more modern days, it was now "up to the Confederates" to pursue their routed enemy to the very utmost. His line of retreat was circuitous and offered us rare opportunity to cut it at Cub Run by a short advance from Stone Bridge; or at Centreville, by an advance of three miles from Mitchell's Ford. Johnston and Beauregard both sent orders to different commands to make such advances, *but neither went in person to supervise and urge forward the execution of the orders, though time was of the very essence.* Both generals and the President spent the valuable hours of daylight still left in riding over the battle-field, as Napoleon lost his opportunity to crush Wellington at Quatre Bras by wasting hours in riding over the field of Ligny. Owing to their absence from the field, the advance from Mitchell's Ford was countermanded by Major Whiting of Johnston's staff, and that from the Stone Bridge, after being first checked, was later countermanded by Beauregard on receipt of a false rumor, which would not have been credited had the orders been in process of execution.

Cautious Orders

It was my fortune to carry the first order checking the pursuit, and my recollection of the circumstances is vivid. When I reached Beauregard, coming from the signal hill, the enemy was in full flight, some retreating across the Stone Bridge and others toward Sudley; and orders were being despatched to different commands concerning the pursuit. Kershaw, with the 7th and 8th S.C. regiments, was ordered to pursue across the Stone Bridge and along Warrenton pike. I accompanied the general in riding over the field and in looking after minor matters for some time. About 6 P.M. I happened to be the only one of his personal staff with him. Rather abruptly, and apropos of nothing that I saw or heard, he said to me: "Ride across the Stone Bridge and find Col. Kershaw, who is conducting the pursuit along the pike. Order him to advance very carefully and not to attack."

I had recently read accounts of the affair at Big Bethel, Va., June 10, in which Magruder had repulsed Butler, whose troops fell back to Fortress Monroe in a panic, though entirely unpursued. I noted two facts: (1) That Magruder's cavalry, which had been ordered to pursue, had allowed itself to be "bluffed" by Greble's U.S. Battery. This was entirely out of ammunition, but it had turned back pursuit of our cavalry by unlimbering [unhitching] their empty guns. (2) That though victorious, Magruder retreated to Yorktown the same afternoon, though perhaps with less haste than was used in Butler's return to Fortress Monroe. It seemed to me now that peremptory orders "not to attack" might result in another such scandal. I hesitated to make any suggestion, remembering army stories of replies by old generals to young aides who had volunteered advice. But I ventured to say: "Shall I tell him not to attack under *any circumstances*, no matter *what* the condition of the enemy in his front?" He replied: "Kemper's battery has been ordered to join him. Let him wait for it to come up. Then he can pursue, but cautiously, and he must not attack unless he has a decided advantage."

Better satisfied, I rode on my errand. A mile beyond the Stone Bridge a member of Congress, Mr. Ely of N.Y., was brought out of the woods a prisoner, as I passed, and turned over to the guard. A half-mile farther I overtook Kershaw forming in line of battle, a Federal gun, near the bridge over Cub Run, having opened fire upon his column. After a few minutes, during which skirmishers were advanced, Kemper's battery arrived and opened fire with two guns on the position at Cub Run.

I then turned back to rejoin Beauregard, and, at the Stone Bridge, met Elzey's brigade coming over. It was now nearly seven o'clock and the sun about a half-hour high when on the Stone Bridge I met Ferguson of Beauregard's staff, bearing orders not only to stop the pursuit, but to recall all troops to the south side of Bull Run. I asked the reason and was answered that a message had been brought to the generals, who were still on the battle-field, that a force of the enemy had been seen south of Bull Run in rear of our right flank. Ferguson pronounced the message as absurd, and was carrying the orders reluctantly. I soon rejoined the two generals upon the field, and among the staff-officers found that no regard was being paid to the story. But the orders already despatched were not recalled, and, until late at night, all the troops on the north side were being brought back.

Meanwhile, Kemper's fire on the bridge at Cub Run had wrecked a team on the bridge, and caused a panic and an inextricable jam of over fifty vehicles, including guns, caissons [ammunition carriages], wagons, and ambulances, from which the drivers had cut many of the teams. Hundreds of the infantry also had thrown their guns into the stream as they crossed the bridge. Here Kershaw was joined by some of our cavalry which had crossed Bull Run at Ball's Ford, and later, by some which had followed the enemy via Sudley. When the orders to return to the south side were received, he left one of his regiments of infantry and this cavalry in charge of the situation. These during the night cleared up the blockade and in the morning brought to Manassas 17 guns, including the 30-pounder Parrott, with over 20 caissons and many other vehicles.

Wasteful Movements

It now only remains of the battle, to give the brief story of the five brigades of our right and centre which held the line of Bull Run, opposite Centreville, and were confronted by Miles with three brigades. Under the confusion of orders in the morning which has been mentioned, Ewell, about 10 A.M. started to cross Bull Run, was recalled; was again sent across and a mile and a half in advance; was again recalled, and, about 2 P.M. was ordered to march to the battle-field. Here he was followed by Holmes. They reached the vicinity of the field after the rout of the enemy. Then, on the false alarm about 6:30 P.M., they were ordered to march back to Union Mills, where they arrived late at night, worn out with dust, heat, and fatigue, without having fired a shot all day.

Next to Ewell and Holmes came Jones, who had crossed early and waited for Ewell, as has been told. He was also recalled about 11 A.M. About noon he was ordered to cross again and to make some demonstrations. He did so and attempted to charge a battery with Jenkins's S.C. regiment, but became entangled in difficult ground under sharp artillery fire. After losing 14 killed and 62 wounded, and finding his effort isolated and hopeless, he fell back. Next to the left of Jones was Longstreet. He also crossed and recrossed Bull Run in the morning, and crossed again about noon as Jones did. In the afternoon about four he was called back to the south side by orders from Johnston. But he had scarcely completed the movement, when, about half-past five, there came from Johnston orders for Bonham and Longstreet to advance upon Centreville and intercept the routed forces from Stone Bridge. Neither of the generals came to see this order executed, and the manner in which it was ignored and disobeyed is instructive. It shows that the giving of orders *to go into action* is but one-half of the duty of a commanding general. . . .

"Never Did an Enemy Make a Cleaner Escape"

On my return from the message to Kershaw I rejoined Beauregard on the field, and was with him until after dark, when I was sent to escort Gen. Johnston back to Manassas Junction by the Sudley-Manassas road. On the road we were overtaken by President Davis with Beauregard and most of his staff. Between 10 and 11 P.M. we all arrived at the headquarters in the village. After supper a conference was held between the President and the two generals in an upper room. While it was in progress, probably about midnight, there arrived Maj. R.C. Hill, a staff-officer in Johnston's command, who had taken part in the pursuit in the afternoon, and who now came to report that he had "made his way into Centreville, and had found it entirely deserted, and the streets blockaded with abandoned artillery and caissons."

This was the first intimation which reached headquarters that the enemy's retreat, even without any pursuit, had degenerated into a panic, and Maj. Hill was taken at once upstairs to make his report in person to the generals and the President. He was well known under the sobriquet of "Crazy Hill," to distinguish him from another Hill, classmate at West Point. Nothing that he had ever done had justified his nickname, but it arose from something peculiar in his eye, tones, and manner, all suggestive of suppressed excitement. As a matter of fact, he had not been to Centreville, but only to Cub Run bridge. He had come upon the field with a company of cavalry, and had seen the blockaded guns and caissons. There was no other such blockade, at Centreville or elsewhere.

The details of what took place in the council, after Hill had told his story and been dismissed, indicate that the case was one where too many cooks spoiled the broth. Immediate advance should have been made. While Hill had not really been at Centreville, an advance there after midnight would have found it nearly if not entirely deserted, and might have overtaken the rear of the retreating Federals. Mr. Davis suggested immediate pursuit, and there was some discussion as to which troops were in best condition and most conveniently situated. Johnston, who was the commander-in-chief, offered no definite motion, and there ensued a pause. Beauregard's adjutant, Col. Jordan, then asked the President if he would dictate an order. He complied and dictated one for immediate pursuit. Conversation began on whether pursuit at dawn would answer, and also as to Hill and his story. It was brought out that Hill was known as "Crazy Hill," and, though no one knew him personally, some doubt was felt, and the order was modified into one directing a reconnaissance at dawn by Bonham's and Cocke's brigades and infantry.

At dawn next morning it was pouring rain and it continued most of the day. This heavy precipitation has often been appealed to by the rain-makers as confirmation of their theories that rain may be induced by heavy cannonading.

The reconnaissances ordered were made and, of course, found the country deserted. Our cavalry followed the retreat beyond Fairfax Court House, and picked up a few stragglers and about 20 wagons. These small matters and the artillery captured at Cub Run and brought in during the day amused and interested us while the last hours of our opportunity passed away. Never did an enemy make a cleaner escape out of such an exposed position after such an utter rout.

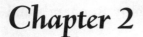

Chapter 2

Early Victories

Chapter Preface

The Confederate army achieved the first victory of the Civil War at the First Battle of Manassas, or Bull Run, which took place in July 1861. While Bull Run bolstered Confederate morale, the continuing inaction of Union general George McClellan provided even more proof to the Southern leaders of their own sound strategies. Seeing McClellan and the federal army and militias camped in the vicinity of Washington, D.C., unable or unwilling to come out for a decisive battle, convinced Southern leaders that the war would soon be over, that their cause was just, and that the Confederacy would prevail.

Early Confederate victories continued during the Peninsula Campaign of 1862, in which Confederate general Joe Johnston stopped a vast Union army that was driving on Richmond along the peninsulas west of Chesapeake Bay. Thomas "Stonewall" Jackson led his Confederate army up the Shenandoah Valley of eastern Virginia, and the Union forces, rent by dissension and political rivalry among its leaders, retreated from Virginia in August. After Johnston was wounded during the Peninsula Campaign, the Confederacy also gained a brilliant new commander in General Robert E. Lee, who organized his regiments into the Army of Northern Virginia and prepared for a final, decisive attack on the former national capital of Washington, D.C.

The war was going well—too well to notice that the South was losing soldiers and equipment that it could barely afford to replace, and that it was fighting to protect its own territory while the farms, industries, and railroads of the wealthier North went untouched. Complacent Southern leaders delayed actions—such as establishing a single currency, raising taxes, and starting military conscription—that could have helped them to finance the war effort and supply their armies. The embargo on cotton, intended to force European nations to ally with the South, only hurt Southern farmers. The skill and obstinacy of Confederate officers had won the first year of the Civil War, but as the conflict dragged on, not even Lee and Jackson would be able to overcome the South's worsening disadvantages.

A Month with "The Rebels"

Anonymous

For Europeans, the Civil War offered great political and military interest. The United States represented an experiment in democracy still largely untried in Europe— and the success or failure of the young nation foretold the problems and possibilities of that experiment in the rest of the world. A key problem for Europe's political leaders was whether or not to recognize the independence of the Confederacy and thus doom the Union. Although powerful landowners and nobility supported the slaveowning South, the European working class by and large supported the industrialized North. The Civil War therefore had a reflection in the old class contests of Europe.

Above it all stood the exciting drama of war itself, which sparked the public's fascination on a continent that had been largely at peace since the defeat of Napoleon at Waterloo in 1815. Leading European journals sent their adventurous correspondents across the Atlantic and into the field to report on the Civil War from both sides of the battlefield. This anonymous account from *Blackwood's Edinburgh Magazine* vividly describes the civilians and soldiers of the Confederacy in the first, most enthusiastic year of the war.

Being disappointed in finding any of that Union feeling in the south of Kentucky of which we had heard so much in New York, we proceeded to Nashville in Tennessee. More camps, more soldiers, more drilling. Men, women, and

Excerpted from "A Month with 'the Rebels,'" anonymous, *Blackwood's Edinburgh Magazine*, December 1861.

children think of nothing but the war. Fathers of large families are frequently seen serving in the ranks as privates, side by side with their sons. Ladies make soldiers' coats and trousers, while children knit their stockings. Trade is in a great measure at a stand-still; but the rapidity with which the people, hitherto dependent upon the North for every manufactured article, however simple, are beginning to supply their wants for themselves, receives at Nashville a curious exemplification. A few weeks ago a boy discovered a method of making percussion-caps, which the army was then much in need of. A factory was forthwith established, that now turns out some millions per week.

Contented Slaves

Amongst the dangers which we had heard at New York threatened the South, a revolt of the slave population was said to be the most imminent. Let us take, then, a peep at a cotton-field, and see what likelihood there is of such a contingency.

On the bank of the Alabama river, which winds its yellow course through dense woods of oak, ash, maple, and pine, thickened with tangled copse of varied evergreens, lie some of the most fertile plantations of the State. One of these we had the advantage of visiting. Its owner received us with all that hospitality and unaffected *bonhommie* which invariably distinguish a Southern gentleman. Having mounted a couple of hacks [carriages], we started off through a large pine-wood, and soon arrived at a "clearing" of about' 200 acres in extent, on most of which was growing an average cotton-crop. This was a fair sample of the rest of the plantation, which consisted altogether of 7000 acres. Riding into the middle of the field, we found ourselves surrounded by about forty slaves, men, women, and children, engaged in "picking." They were all well dressed, and seemed happy and cheerful. Wishing to know what time of day it was, I asked Mr.—— the hour; whereupon one of the darkies by my side took out a gold watch and informed me.

"Do your labourers generally wear gold watches, sir?" I inquired.

"A great many of them have. Why, sir, my negroes all have their cotton-plots and gardens, and most of them little orchards."

We found from their own testimony that they are fed well, chiefly upon pork, corn, potatoes, and rice, carefully attended to when sick, and Sundays dress better than their masters.

Many of them had six or seven hundred dollars of their own, which they either lend to the banks or hide in the ground. In the hot weather they begin work at six in the morning, and go on till ten; they then go home till about three, and, when the sun declines, return to their work till six or seven. In the cool weather they begin soon after daylight, and rest for two or three hours in the middle of the day.

We next visited the "Station," a street of cottages in a pine-wood, where 'Mr.———'s "family" reside. These we found clean and comfortable. Two of the men were sick, and had been visited that morning by a doctor; in the mean time they were looked after by the nurses of the establishment, of whom there were three to take care of the children and invalids.

On the whole, it can fearlessly be said, if this is a true type of the mode in which slaves are treated in the South, that their physical condition is as good, if not better, than that of any labouring population in the world. The masters ridicule the idea of disloyalty. They live amongst them in the most perfect confidence, and never bestow a serious thought upon what they consider such an impossibility as a "negro insurrection." Having visited other plantations in Alabama, South Carolina, and Georgia, we cannot resist the belief that the great mass of the slaves in the South must be pronounced to be well cared for and contented; and although there are necessarily a thousand things connected with "the institution" of which no Englishman can approve, it is undoubtedly true that, notwithstanding the strenuous efforts of abolitionists, the negroes bear the yoke cheerfully, and heartily join their fortunes to those of their masters in the great struggle in which they are now engaged.

Many plantations may now be seen without a white man upon them, except the overseers; and instances occur daily of the fidelity with which "servants" who have accompanied their masters to the war serve them in the camp and field. Further, the generals employ the negroes in the commissariat, and upon earthworks in situations where desertion and consequent freedom would be perfectly easy, thereby showing in the slaves a confidence which is justified by the fact that the Northern army, now on Arlington Heights, find it almost impossible to obtain correct information of what is going on in the Confederate camp, two miles distant from the Union outposts.

A Just Cause

The perfect unanimity throughout the whole South in the belief that their cause is just, strikes the stranger as one of the most formidable symptoms which the Union has to fear. Without pretending to form an opinion as to whether this universal conviction is rightly or wrongly arrived at, we simply assert the fact. The same story is told in the trains, in the hotels, on the plantations, in the drawing-rooms, in the camps, and in the newspapers, by young and old, rich and poor, men and women, with a uniformity that would be monotonous, were it not for the fire generally thrown into its narration.

They say that the North began the conflict years ago, in the irritating and unprovoked agitation of the slavery question, and have continued it from the time of the Missouri controversy [Compromise of 1820] to the 4th of last March, when the President announced that the platform of his party was "a law unto him," and that party had declared there was an "irrepressible conflict" between the two sections of the Union. If we remarked that slavery was an evil about which we considered all American statesmen must feel anxiety, they replied, The President was sworn to defend it. It is an institution which feeds and clothes the world, which protects the negro against the vicissitudes of old age, sickness, and infancy, and keeps him in the only position where he can be useful to society, and harmless to himself. That the sun fixed the boundaries between white and black labour, in spite of arms and laws; and so sure as one flourished in Massachusetts, the other would prosper in Georgia. That when the North abolished slavery, and sold their slaves to the South, they then turned round, broke faith, and endeavoured to disquiet a title emanating from themselves.

That the tariff laws were ruinous to the South. That in raising their revenue by heavy duties on foreign goods, which came back in return for Southern produce, the North were making the South pay the great bulk of the expense of government.

That by prohibiting trade in foreign ships, the South were obliged to take Northern to the exclusion of foreign goods.

That, by monopolising the European trade, the North obtained great profits in brokerage and in freights upon Southern produce to Europe, as well as upon European goods brought back in return for that produce, from all of which the South reaped little benefit. . . .

The women of all classes seemed not less unanimous and devoted than the men. Along the line of railway crowds waved flowers and handkerchiefs as the train bore towards the seat of war those who were nearest to their affections. Mothers, sisters, wives, flocked to the railway stations to bid farewell to those for whom they would willingly give their lives. Yet few shed tears at these partings. All the weaker feelings of their nature seemed sealed up or banished; and a conviction that each was making a sacrifice in a holy cause was stamped on every countenance.

In passing along the line of railway, between Montgomery and Charleston, we had many opportunities of conversing with the soldiers in the trains; these were representatives of every class in the country—planters, lawyers, shopkeepers, and even clergymen. Our conversation was generally quickly courted, and questions eagerly asked as to our opinion upon the war.

But "conspicuous by their absence" were the farmer-boys—a body from which the best of the Northern army are recruited. In the South, of course, this class does not exist, the whole of the field-labour being carried on by slaves. This industrial peculiarity, which was considered by foreigners as the great weakness of the Confederates, has hitherto proved to them a tower of strength. We found in all the States which we visited, agricultural operations progressing with as much vigour and regularity as in times of profound peace. Indeed, tracts of land hitherto allowed to run waste will this year be sown in corn to counteract as much as pos-

---

The Civil War: A Marxist Interpretation

Karl Marx and Friedrich Engels, architects of revolutionary socialism, had their own particular slant on the progress of the Civil War. In Marxist thinking, all events and actions could be understood in the light of the ongoing world revolution that would sweep away the old, capitalist structures and replace them with a government by and for the world's industrial workers. They corresponded on the very subject in the summer of 1862, when Confederate successes on the battlefield were convincing many European observers that the war would result in a victory of the slaveowning class.

Engels to Marx:

July 30, 1862

Things go wrong in America. . . . What cowardice in government and Congress! They are afraid of conscription, of resolute financial steps, of attacks on slavery, of everything that is urgently necessary; they let everything loaf along as it will, and if the semblance of some measure finally gets through Congress, the honorable Lincoln so qualifies it that nothing at all is left of it any longer. This slackness, this collapse like a punctured pig's bladder, under the pressure of defeats that have annihilated one army, the strongest and best, and actually left Washington exposed, this total absence of any elasticity in the whole mass of the people—this proves to me that it is all up. . . .

For the South, on the contrary—it's no use shutting one's eyes to the fact—it's a matter of bloody earnest. That we get

sible the inconvenience of the [Union] blockade [of Southern ports].

Self-Reliance

But the slaves are not employed exclusively in out-door labour. Necessity has taught the South that she must rely upon herself for many things which she cannot do without, and which, in former times, it was cheaper to import than to

---

no cotton is already one proof. The guerrillas in the border states are a second. But that after being thus shut off from the world, an agricultural people can sustain such a war and after severe defeats and losses in resources, men and territory, can nevertheless now stand forth as the victor and threaten to carry its offensive right into the North, this is in my opinion decisive. . . . If the North does not proceed forthwith in revolutionary fashion, it will get an ungodly hiding and deserve it—and it looks like it.

Marx to Engels:

August 7, 1862

I do not altogether share your views on the American Civil War. I do not think that all is up. . . . The Southerners . . . acted as one man from the beginning. The North itself has turned the slaves into a military force on the side of the Southerners, instead of turning it against them. The South leaves productive labor to the slaves and could therefore put its whole fighting strength in the field without disturbance. The South had unified military leadership, the North had not. . . . In my opinion all this will take another turn. In the end the North will make war seriously, adopt revolutionary methods and throw over the domination of the border slave statesmen. . . . The Northwest and New England wish to and will force the government to give up the diplomatic method of conducting war which it has used hitherto. . . . If Lincoln does not give way (which he will do, however) there will be a revolution.

Belle Becker Sideman and Lillian Friedman, *Europe Looks at the Civil War.* New York: The Orion Press, 1960.

manufacture. Large numbers of hand-looms and spinning-wheels are seen in the country districts, which the population are rapidly learning to make good use of; and we met one planter who showed us enough cloth for the uniforms of fifty men, that had been entirely made on his own property.

Again, before the war, leather was so little manufactured in the South, that hides were seldom saved, and tan-yards were almost unknown. Shoemaking, saddlery, and many other industrial employments, are now being quickly brought into operation; and all the country appears to want is the machinery to adapt its boundless natural productions to the wants of man. The blockade has undoubtedly been productive of great individual inconvenience. All communication by letter has been cut off. Friends are unable to correspond. Painful instances are met with every day of the anxiety to hear tidings of relatives abroad. But we doubt very much whether it has at all materially crippled the South, while nothing has more served to effect that social separation which the people take pleasure in, declaring it is as complete now as if the Confederacy had been established for fifty years. . . .

A Visit to the Army

Having been kindly provided with a pass to the headquarters of one of the generals near Manassas, about a hundred and twenty miles from Richmond, we were allowed to go up in a soldiers' train. All along the line we found flags waving from the houses, and crowds assembled at the stations to bid God-speed to those who were leaving home, family, and profession for the rough realities of active warfare. . . .

The country for many miles around Manassas is hill and dale, covered naturally with dense hardwood of various kinds, which is cleared away from time to time, leaving patches of open ground, varying in size from two to a hundred acres; but few of these spaces are greater in extent than the Green Park in London, whilst some of them are much less. Altogether the character of the district would not be unlike that of the neighbourhood of Bromley in Kent [in England], if the latter were more extensively wooded, and less generally cultivated. Through the valleys run numerous streams, the largest being Bull's Run, a winding but somewhat sluggish river, about forty feet wide; varying in depth from two to eight feet, with rocky banks on each side, which in some places are quite perpendicular. The different camps are scattered about through this great wooded tract in strong positions, but so little seen are they, that frequently, when galloping down a narrow pathway, we would find ourselves in the midst of tents and soldiers almost before we could pull up our horses.

The first thing that struck us in riding through the country was the respect which is everywhere shown for the rights of property. Gentlemen's villas lie along roads over which many thousand soldiers daily pass, and we never saw a piece of paling hurt or a garden intruded upon; and in the villages the poultry and pigs are running about as in times of profound peace. . . .

A Multicultural Confederacy

The *personnel* of the army is very varied. For instance, in the Louisiana regiments are seen the bronzed and fiery-eyed French creoles mingled with many Irish and native Americans from New Orleans. The Alabamans, proud of their gallant 4th, their flying artillery and other regiments, may be known by their strong frames, gay manners, and devil-may-care air. The South Carolinians, sallow in complexion, tall in stature, seldom need the Palmetto to tell the stranger the State from which they come; but in all regiments it is easy to perceive differences in manner and bearing, indicative of the various classes of which the army is composed.

Numbers of wealthy planters serve as privates side by side with the professional man, the shopkeeper, the clerk, the labourer; and all go through the ordinary fatigue duties incident to camp-life. We saw a poor negro servant actually shedding tears because his master, on being told off to dig a trench round a battery, would not allow him "to lend a hand."

"'Twill nebber do, massa," he said; "I go 'tarnal mad wid dem darn'd Yankees."

One day we heard a lad boasting to one of a different regiment of the number of gentlemen in his company who had thousands of dollars at their command. The latter replied, "Oh, of course they fight; but we have some in ours who have not got a cent!" The Washington artillery, comprising many batteries, is composed of the best blood in New Orleans. The gunners, dressed in light-blue uniforms, are all men of independent means. General Beauregard's son, for instance, left his father's staff, and entered as a private. The drivers are regularly enlisted into the army, and paid by the regiment; so here is a force which does not cost the country a single farthing. Their efficiency is undoubted, and the execution which they did at Bull's Run, has led to their material augmentation, and the formation of others on similar principles. From the same city comes a very different regiment, called the New Orleans "Zouaves," dressed in red caps, blue braided jackets, and trousers striped with light grey and red. These men look like pirates—bearded, fierce-looking fellows—

"Theirs to believe no prey, no plan amiss."

Apparently at least; for as they marched past the General with a long swinging step, singing a wild martial air, we thought they were as formidable a body of men as we should care to see.

The drill of the army is the same as the French, the step even quicker than the Zouaves, and a good deal longer than that of the English infantry. Movements are executed with considerable precision, and as rapidly as in English light-infantry battalions.

From the reports we had heard in the North, we expected to find ragged and half-clad regiments; instead of which we failed, during many rides through the various camps, to see one man who was not clad in serviceable attire. It was expected that winter clothing would be served out before the

1st of November, and that dress would then become more uniform.

But the point to which the chief attention of officers and men is directed is the arms. Besides the Enfield rifle, most of the privates in the army carry at least one revolver and a bowie-knife: these are invariably kept bright and in good condition; and the early training which all Southerners undergo in shooting squirrels as soon as they are able to handle a gun, gives them a facility of using their weapons and a correctness of aim that renders their fire unusually formidable. . . .

Our Sympathies

The time which we had allowed ourselves for our American tour being now nearly spent, we returned to New York, where we found most persons altogether in ignorance of the feelings and intentions of the South; and so strong is the confidence generally reposed in the numerical strength of their vast army, the alleged efficiency of the navy, and the great wealth of the New England States, that few persons are to be met with who think gloomily of the future. . . .

In these islands [Great Britain], of course, we all pray for universal emancipation. We have made enormous sacrifices in the cause ourselves; but we cannot help sympathising with ten millions of people struggling for independence; nor can we think that the condition of the negro in the Southern States will remain long what it now is, but that, if European intercourse be established with the Confederacy, and she be admitted into the family of nations, commerce, always favourable to freedom, will then gradually but surely effect far more humane results than those which the most sincere Abolitionists can ever attain.

The Ride Around McClellan

John Esten Cooke

In the early summer of 1862, the Confederate army found itself in southeastern Virginia, defending Richmond against a much larger Union force. The Union army under George B. McClellan had been transported by ship to a peninsula of land that stretched from the mouth of the Rappahannock River to the southern capital. Although McClellan had the advantage, he was reluctant to attack because he overestimated the size of the Rebel army around Richmond. Instead the Confederates mounted a surprise assault which was played out in a series of bloody but indecisive battles.

John Esten Cooke, a distinguished Southern writer, took part in this Peninsula Campaign in the company of General James Ewell Brown ("Jeb") Stuart, a brilliant Confederate cavalry commander. On June 12, 1862, Stuart was ordered by the new Southern commander, Robert E. Lee, to make a reconnaissance of the Union army's right flank, in preparation for a Confederate attack that would drive McClellan back north. But instead of merely scouting and skirmishing, Stuart led his cavalry companies completely around and behind McClellan, raiding, burning, and fighting along the way. As the novelist Cooke tells the story, Stuart's famous "Ride Around McClellan" was a dashing adventure.

Who that went with Stuart on his famous "Ride around McClellan" in the summer of 1862, just before the bloody battles of the Chickahominy, will ever forget the fun,

Excerpted from "Stuart's 'Ride Around McClellan,'" in *Wearing of the Gray*, by John Esten Cooke (n.p., 1862).

the frolic, the romance—and the peril too—of that fine journey? Thinking of the gay ride now, when a century seems to have swept between that epoch and the present, I recall every particular, live over every emotion. Once more I hear the ringing laugh of Stuart, and see the keen flash of the blue eyes under the black feather of the prince of cavaliers!

If the reader will follow me he shall see what took place on this rapid ride, witness some incidents of this first and king of raids. The record will be that of an eye-witness, and the personal prominence of the writer must be excused as inseparable from the narrative. I need not dwell upon the "situation" in June, 1862. All the world knows that, at that time, McClellan had advanced with his magnificent army [the Army of the Potomac] of 156,000 men, to the banks of the Chickahominy, and pushing across, had fought on the last day of May the bloody but indecisive battle of the Seven Pines. On the right it was a Confederate, on the left a Federal success; and General McClellan drew back, marshalled his great lines, darkening both the northern and southern banks of the Chickahominy, and prepared for a more decisive blow at the Confederate capital, whose spires were in sight. Before him, however, lay the Southern army, commanded now by Lee, who had succeeded Johnston, wounded in the fight of "Seven Pines." The moment was favourable for a heavy attack by Lee. . . .

It was considered a better plan to attack the Federal army on the north bank of the Chickahominy, drive it from its works, and try the issue in the fields around Cold Harbour. The great point was to ascertain if this was practicable, and especially to find what defences, if any, the enemy had to guard the approach to their right wing. If these were slight, the attack could be made with fair prospects of success. [General Stonewall] Jackson could sweep around while Lee assailed the lines near Mechanicsville; then one combined assault would probably defeat the Federal force. To find the character of the enemy's works beyond the stream—his positions and movements—General Stuart was directed to take a portion of his cavalry, advance as far as Old Church, if practicable, and then be guided by circumstances. Such were the orders with which Stuart set out about moonrise on the night, I think, of June 12, upon this dangerous expedition.

A Thundering Gallop

As the young cavalier mounted his horse on that moonlight night he was a gallant figure to look at. The gray coat buttoned to the chin; the light French sabre balanced by the pistol in its black holster; the cavalry boots above the knee, and the brown hat with its black plume floating above the bearded features, the brilliant eyes, and the huge moustache, which curled with laughter at the slightest provocation—these made Stuart the perfect picture of a gay cavalier, and the spirited horse he rode seemed to feel that he carried one whose motto was to "do or die." I chanced to be his sole companion as he galloped over the broad field near his headquarters, and the glance of the blue eyes of Stuart at that moment was as brilliant as the lightning itself.

Catching up with his column of about 1500 horsemen, and two pieces of horse-artillery under Colonels William H.F. Lee, Fitz Lee, and Will.T. Martin, of Mississippi—cavalier as brave as ever drew sabre—Stuart pushed on northward as if going to join Jackson, and reaching the vicinity of Taylorsville, near Hanover Junction, went that night into bivouac. He embraced the opportunity, after midnight, of riding with Colonel W.H.F. Lee to "Hickory Hill," the residence of Colonel Williams Wickham—afterward General Wickham—who had been recently wounded and paroled. Here he went to sleep in his chair after talking with Colonel Wickham, narrowly escaped capture from the enemy rear, and returning before daylight, advanced with his column straight upon Hanover Court-House. Have you ever visited this picturesque spot, reader? We looked upon it on that day of June—upon its old brick court-house, where Patrick Henry made his famous speech against the parsons, its ancient tavern, its modest roofs, the whole surrounded by the fertile fields waving with golden grain—all this we looked at with unusual interest. For in this little bird's nest, lost as it were in a sea of rippling wheat and waving foliage, some "Yankee cavalry" had taken up their abode; their horses stood ready saddled in the street, and this dark mass we now gazed at furtively from behind a wooden knoll, in rear of which Stuart's column was drawn up ready to move at the word. Before he gave the signal, the General dispatched Colonel Fitz Lee round to the right, to flank and cut off the party. But all at once the scouts in front were descried by the enemy; shots resounded; and seeing that his presence was discovered, Stuart gave the word, and swept at a thundering gallop down the hill. The startled "blue birds," as we used to call our Northern friends, did not wait; the squadron on picket at the court-house, numbering some one hundred and fifty men, hastily got to horse—then presto! they disappear in a dense cloud of dust from which echo some parting salutes from their carbines. Stuart pressed on rapidly, took the road to Old Church, and near a place called Hawes' Shop, in a thickly wooded spot, was suddenly charged himself. It did not amount to much, and seemed rather an attempt at reconnaissance. A Federal officer at the head of a detachment came on at full gallop, very nearly ran into the head of our column, and then seeing the dense mass of gray coats, fired his pistol, wheeled short about, and went back at full speed, with his detachment.

Stuart had given, in his ringing voice, the order: "Form fours! draw sabre! charge!" and now the Confederate people pursued at headlong speed, uttering shouts and yells sufficiently loud to awaken the seven sleepers! The men were evidently exhilarated by the chase, the enemy just keeping near enough to make an occasional shot practicable. A considerable number of the Federal cavalrymen were overtaken and captured, and these proved to belong to the company in which Colonel Fitz Lee had formerly been a lieutenant. I could not refrain from laughter at the pleasure which "Colonel Fitz"— whose motto should be *toujours gai* ["always happy"]— seemed to take in inquiring after his old cronies. "Was Brown alive? where was Jones? and was Robinson sergeant still?" Colonel Fitz never stopped until he found out everything. The prisoners laughed as they recognised him. Altogether, reader, the interview was the most friendly imaginable.

A Bloody Awakening at Shiloh

Many Confederate and Union soldiers had their first taste of battle at Shiloh, on April 6, 1862. In the lore of Civil War infantry, Shiloh was one of the worst fights of the war—not only for its high casualties, but also for the way it destroyed the myth of gallant combat, a myth that had driven many soldiers to volunteer for service in the first place. In his tour through the Confederate legends of the modern South, Confederates in the Attic, *author Tony Horwitz sums up the tragedy of Shiloh.*

The day dawned just as it had on April 6th in 1862— "clear, beautiful and still," in the words of Sam Watkins, a Confederate private who wrote a famous memoir about the War called *Co. Aytch.* It was at Shiloh that Watkins experienced his first true taste of battle—"seeing the elephant," as Civil War soldiers called it. Fully 86 percent of rebels at Shiloh and 60 percent of Federals had never seen the elephant before. Advancing toward what Watkins called the "bang, boom, whirr-siz-siz-siz" of battle, he saw many of his comrades stricken with loose bowels, and glimpsed one man shooting off a finger to avoid the fight. Watkins's own bravado faltered at a field littered with dead and wounded. "I must confess that I never realized the 'pomp and circumstance' of the thing called glorious war until I saw this," he wrote.

A staggering number of soldiers at Shiloh would never see the elephant again. One in four became casualties of the two-day battle, and the toll on both sides—24,000 in all— surpassed the *combined* American casualties in the Revolutionary War, the War of 1812, and the Mexican War. This "grim arithmetic," as [Civil War historian] Shelby Foote called it, sobered those both North and South who thought the War would end quickly and with little bloodshed.

Tony Horwitz, *Confederates in the Attic.* New York: Pantheon Books, 1998.

Death on Horseback

The gay chase continued until we reached the Tottapotamoi, a sluggish stream, dragging its muddy waters slowly between rush-clad banks, beneath drooping trees; and this was crossed by a small rustic bridge. The line of the stream was entirely undefended by works; the enemy's right wing was unprotected; Stuart had accomplished the object of his expedition, and afterward piloted Jackson over this very same road. But to continue the narrative of his movement: The picket at the bridge had been quickly driven in, and disappeared at a gallop, and on the high ground beyond, Colonel W.H.F. Lee, who had taken the front, encountered the enemy. The force appeared to be about a regiment, and they were drawn up in line of battle in the fields to receive our attack. It came without delay. Placing himself at the head of his horsemen, Colonel Lee swept forward at the *pas de charge* ["charging pace"], and with shouts the two lines came together. The shock was heavy, and the enemy—a portion of the old United States Regulars, commanded by Captain Royal—stood their ground bravely, meeting the attack with the sabre. Swords clashed, pistols and carbines banged, yells, shouts, cheers resounded; then the Federal line was seen to give back, and take to headlong flight. They were pursued with ardour, and the men were wild with this—to many of them—their first fight. But soon after all joy disappeared from their faces, at sight of a spectacle which greeted them. Captain Latanè, of the Essex cavalry, had been mortally wounded in the charge, and as the men of his company saw him lying bloody before them, many a bearded face was wet with tears. The scene at his grave afterward became the subject of Mr. Washington's picture, "The Burial of Latanè;" and in his general order after the expedition, Stuart called upon his command to take for their watchword in the future "*Avenge Latanè!*" Captain Royal, the Federal commandant, had also been badly wounded, and many of his force killed. I remember passing a Dutch cavalryman who was writhing with a bullet through the breast, and bit-ing and tearing up the ground. He called for water, and I directed a servant at a house near by to bring him some. The last I saw of him, a destitute cavalryman was taking off his spurs as he was dying. War is a hard trade.

Fitz Lee immediately pressed on and burst into the camp near Old Church, where large supplies of boots, pistols, liquors, and other commodities were found. These were speedily appropriated by the men, and the tents were set on fire amid loud shouts. The spectacle was animating; but a report having got abroad that one of the tents contained powder, the vicinity thereof was evacuated in almost less than no time. We were now at Old Church, where Stuart was to be guided in his further movements by circumstances. I looked at him; he was evidently reflecting. In a moment he turned round to me and said: "Tell Fitz Lee to come along, I'm going to move on with my column." These words terminated my doubt, and I understood in an instant that the General had decided on the bold and hazardous plan of passing entirely round McClellan's army.

"I think the quicker we move now the better," I said, with a laugh.

"Right," was Stuart's reply; "tell the column to move on at a trot."

So at a rapid trot the column moved.

Circling McClellan

The gayest portion of the raid now began. From this moment it was neck or nothing, do or die. We had one chance of escape against ten of capture or destruction.

Stuart had decided upon his course with that rapidity, good judgment, and decision, which were the real secrets of his splendid efficiency as a leader of cavalry, in which capacity I believe that he has never been surpassed, either in the late war or any other. He was now in the very heart of the enemy's citadel, with their enormous masses upon every side. He had driven in their advanced force, passed within sight of the white tents of General McClellan's headquarters, burned their camps, and ascertained all that he wished. How was he to return? He could not cross the Pamunkey, and make a circuit back; he had no pontoons [artificial, temporary bridges]. He could not return over the route by which he had advanced. As events afterward showed, the alarm had been given, and an overpowering force of infantry, cavalry, and artillery had been rapidly moved in that direction to intercept the daring raider. Capture stared him in the face, on both of these routes—across the Pamunkey, or back as he came; he must find some other loophole of escape.

Such was the dangerous posture of affairs, and such was the important problem which Stuart decided in five minutes. He determined to make the complete circuit of McClellan's army; and crossing the Chickahominy below Long Bridge, re-enter the Confederate lines from Charles City. If on his way he encountered cavalry he intended to fight it; if a heavy force of infantry barred his way he would elude, or cut a path through it; if driven to the wall and debarred from escape he did not mean to surrender. A few days afterward I said to him:

Confederate general "Jeb" Stuart

"That was a tight place at the river, General. If the enemy had come down on us, you would have been compelled to have surrendered."

"No," was his reply; "one other course was left."

"What was that?"

"To *die game*."

And I know that such was his intention. When a commander means to die game rather than surrender he is a dangerous adversary.

From Old Church onward it was *terra incognita* [unknown ground]. What force of the enemy barred the road was a question of the utmost interest, but adventure of some description might be safely counted on. In about twenty-four hours I, for one, expected either to be laughing with my friends within the Southern lines, or dead, or captured. Which of these three results would follow, seemed largely to depend upon the "chapter of accidents." At a steady trot now, with drawn sabres and carbines ready, the cavalry, followed by the horse-artillery, which was not used during the whole expedition, approached Tunstall's Station on the York River railroad, the enemy's direct line of communication with his base of supplies at the "White House."

Everywhere the ride was crowded with incident. The scouting and flanking parties constantly picked up stragglers, and overhauled unsuspecting wagons filled with the most tempting stores. In this manner a wagon, stocked with champagne and every variety of wines, belonging to a General of the Federal army, fell a prey to the thirsty gray-backs. Still they pressed on. Every moment an attack was expected in front or rear. Colonel Will. T. Martin commanded the latter. "Tell Colonel Martin," Stuart said to me, "to have his artillery ready, and look out for an attack at any moment." I had delivered the message and was riding to the front again, when suddenly a loud cry arose of "Yankees in the rear!" Every sabre flashed, fours were formed, the men wheeled about, when all at once a stunning roar of laughter ran along the line; it was a *canard* [lie]. The column moved up again with its flanking parties well out. The men composing the latter were, many of them, from the region, and for the first time for months saw their mothers and sisters. These went quite wild at sight of their sons and brothers. They laughed and cried, and on the appearance of the long gray column instead of the familiar blue coats of the Federal cavalry, they clapped their hands and fell into ecstasies of delight. One young lady was seen to throw her arms around a brother she had not before met for a long time, bursting into alternate sobs and laughter.

A Keg of Whiskey

The column was now skirting the Pamunkey, and a detachment hurried off to seize and burn two or three transports lying in the river. Soon a dense cloud rose from them, the flames soared up, and the column pushed on. Everywhere were seen the traces of flight—for the alarm of "hornets in the hive" was given. Wagons had turned over, and were abandoned—from others the excellent army stores had been hastily thrown. This writer got a fine red blanket, and an excellent pair of cavalry pantaloons, for which he still owes the United States. Other things lay about in tempting array, but we were approaching Tunstall's, where the column would doubtless make a charge; and to load down a weary horse was injudicious. The advance guard was now in sight of the railroad. There was no question about the affair before us. The column must cut through, whatever force guarded the railroad; to reach the lower Chickahominy the guard here must be overpowered. Now was the time to use the artillery, and every effort was made to hurry it forward. But alas! it had got into a tremendous mudhole, and the wheels were buried to the axle. The horses were lashed, and jumped, almost breaking the traces; the drivers swore; the harness cracked—but the guns did not move. "Gat! Lieutenant," said a sergeant of Dutch origin to the brave Lieutenant McGregor, "it can't be done. But just put that keg on the gun, Lieutenant," pointing, as he spoke, to a keg of whiskey in an ambulance, the spoil of the Federal camp, "and tell the men they can have it if they only pull through!" McGregor laughed, and the keg was quickly perched on the gun. Then took place an exhibition of herculean muscularity which would have delighted Guy Livingston. With eyes fixed ardently upon the keg, the powerful cannoneers waded into the mudhole up to their knees, seized the wheels of gun and caisson loaded down with ammunition, and just simply lifted the whole out, and put them on firm ground. The piece whirled on—the keg had been dismounted—the cannoneers revelled in the spoils they had earned.

Tunstall's was now nearly in sight, and that good fellow

Captain Frayser, afterward Stuart's signal officer, came back and reported one or two companies of infantry at the railroad. Their commander had politely beckoned to him as he reconnoitred, exclaiming in wheedling accents, full of Teutonic blandishment, "Koom yay!" But this cordial invitation was disregarded! Frayser galloped back and reported, and the ringing voice of Stuart ordered "Form platoons! draw sabre! charge!" At the word the sabres flashed, a thundering shout arose, and sweeping on in column of platoons, the gray people fell upon their blue adversaries, gobbling them up, almost without a shot. It was here that my friend Major F—— got the hideous little wooden pipe he used to smoke afterward. He had been smoking a meerschaum when the order to charge was given; and in the rush of the horsemen, dropped and lost it. He now wished to smoke, and seeing that the captain of the Federal infantry had just filled his pipe, leaned down from the saddle, and politely requested him to surrender it.

"I want to smoke!" growled the Federal captain.

"So do I," retorted Major F——.

"This pipe is my property," said the captain.

"Oh! what a mistake!" responded the major politely, as he gently took the small affair and inserted it between his lips. Anything more hideous than the carved head upon it I never saw.

The men swarmed upon the railroad. Quick axes were applied to the telegraph poles, which crashed down, and Redmond Burke went in command of a detachment to burn a small bridge on the railroad near. Suddenly in the midst of the tumult was heard the shrill whistle of a train coming from the direction of the Chickahominy. Stuart quickly drew up his men in a line on the side of the road, and he had no sooner done so than the train came slowly round a wooded bend, and bore down. When within two hundred yards it was ordered to halt, but the command was not obeyed. The engineer crowded on all steam; the train rushed on, and then a thundering volley was opened upon the "flats" containing officers and men. The engineer was shot by Captain Farley, of Stuart's staff, and a number of the soldiers were wounded. The rest threw themselves upon their faces; the train rushed headlong by like some frightened monster bent upon escape, and in an instant it had disappeared.

Stuart then reflected for a single moment. The question was, should he go back and attack the White House, where enormous stores were piled up? It was tempting, and he afterwards told me he could scarcely resist it. But a considerable force of infantry was posted there; the firing had doubtless given them the alarm; and the attempt was too hazardous. The best thing for that gray column was to set their faces toward home, and "keep moving," well closed up both day and night, for the lower Chickahominy. So Stuart pushed on. Beyond the railroad appeared a world of wagons, loaded with grain and coffee—standing in the road abandoned. Quick work was made of them. They were all set on fire, and their contents destroyed. From the horse-trough of one I rescued a small volume bearing on the fly-leaf the name of a young lady of Williamsburg. I think it was a volume of poems—poetic wagon-drivers!

These wagons were only the "vaunt couriers"—the advance guard—of the main body. In a field beyond the stream thirty acres were covered with them. They were all burned. The roar of the soaring flames was like the sound of a forest on fire. How they roared and crackled! The sky overhead, when night had descended, was bloody-looking in the glare.

"Halt! Who Goes There?"

Meanwhile the main column had moved on, and I was riding after it, when I heard the voice of Stuart in the darkness exclaiming with strange agitation:

"Who is here?"

"I am," I answered; and as he recognised my voice he exclaimed:

"Good! where is Rooney Lee?"

"I think he has moved on, General."

"Do you *know* it?" came in the same agitated tone.

"No, but I believe it."

"Will you *swear to it*? I must know! He may take the wrong road, and the column will get separated!"

"I will ascertain if he is in front."

"Well, do so; but take care—you will be captured!"

I told the General I would "gallop on for ever till I found him," but I had not gone two hundred yards in the darkness when hoof-strokes in front were heard, and I ordered:

"Halt! who goes there?"

"Courier, from Colonel William Lee."

"Is he in front?"

"About a mile, sir."

"Good!" exclaimed the voice of Stuart, who had galloped up; and I never heard in human accents such an expression of relief. If the reader of this has ever commanded cavalry, moving at night in an enemy's country, he will understand why Stuart drew that long, deep breath, and uttered that brief word, "Good!" Once separated from the main column and lost—good-by then to Colonel Lee!

Pushing on by large hospitals which were not interfered with, we reached at midnight the three or four houses known as Talleysville; and here a halt was ordered to rest men and horses, and permit the artillery to come up. This pause was fatal to a sutler's [grocery and dry goods] store from which the owners had fled. It was remorselessly ransacked and the edibles consumed. This historian ate in succession figs, beef-tongue, pickle, candy, tomato catsup, preserves, lemons, cakes, sausages, molasses, crackers and canned meats. In presence of these attractive commodities the spirits of many rose. Those who in the morning had made me laugh by saying "General Stuart is going to get his command destroyed—this movement is mad," now regarded Stuart as the first of men; the raid as a feat of splendour and judicious daring which could not fail in terminating successfully. Such is the difference in the views of the military machine, unfed and fed.

Victory at Fredericksburg

Robert Stiles

After a Confederate advance was stopped at Antietam Creek, Maryland, in September 1862, General Lee pulled his Confederate army back across the Potomac River and into Virginia. It was the perfect opportunity for a northern counterattack—but one never came. While the Southerners regrouped, Union General McClellan stood his ground. His indecisiveness angered President Lincoln, who replaced him in November with General Ambrose Burnside.

Burnside soon ordered an all-out attack on Virginia and Richmond. At the Rappahannock River town of Fredericksburg, the Confederate army dug into a steep, fortified hillside known as Marye's Heights. Burnside ordered an attack on the Heights that turned out to be a colossal, bloody failure—a tremendous waste of effort and life that reminds many Civil War historians of the futile trench warfare of World War I.

Robert Stiles, a major of artillery in the Army of Northern Virginia, witnessed the battle firsthand from the heights above Fredericksburg. His account reveals a poetic but clear-eyed view of war and its effects on military men as well as on the hapless civilians often caught in the terrifying crossfire.

In a few days, everything appearing to be quiet at the front, we were sent down into Caroline County [Virginia], along and near the R.F.& P. Railroad, to go into camp for the winter. We selected an ideal position, went vigorously to work

Excerpted from *Four Years Under Marse Robert*, by Robert Stiles (New York: Neale Publishing, 1910).

and built the very best shelters for our horses and cabins for ourselves that we ever put up anywhere; but hardly had they been completed, tried, pronounced eminently satisfactory and christened "Sleepy Hollow," when orders came for us to return at once to Fredericksburg, and that through a blizzard of most inclement weather. Of course we went, and without delay—I cannot say absolutely without grumbling. Indeed the right to grumble is the only civil, political, or social right left to the soldier, and he stands much in his own light if he does not exercise it to the full. We found rather an uncomfortable and forbidding location selected for us outside of Fredericksburg, and we were in a temper too bad to do much for its improvement, so that, as to external conditions, we had rather a hard, comfortless winter; though, even as to these, we perhaps did better than the commands who were ordered to the front later.

The next incident of interest was the bombardment of the old town, but I do not care to enlarge upon this. Really I saw then and see now no justification for it. True the town was occupied by armed men,—Barksdale and his men, our old brigade,—but then the fire did not drive them out; in the nature of things, and especially of the Mississippi brigade, of course it would not, but it did drive out the women and children, many of them. I never saw a more pitiful procession than they made trudging through the deep snow after the warning was given and as the hour drew near. I saw little children tugging along with their doll babies,—some bigger than they were,—but holding their feet up carefully above the snow, and women so old and feeble that they could carry nothing and could barely hobble themselves. There were women carrying a baby in one arm and its bottle, its clothes, and its covering in the other. Some had a Bible and a tooth brush in one hand, a picked chicken and a bag of flour in the other. Most of them had to cross a creek swollen with winter rains, and deadly cold with winter ice and snow. We took the battery horses down and ferried them over, taking one child in front and two behind and sometimes a woman or a girl on either side with her feet in the stirrups, holding on by our shoulders. Where they were going we could not tell, and I doubt if they could. . . .

The Foundling of the 21st Mississippi

Buck Denman,—our old friend Buck, of Leesburg and Fort Johnston fame,—a Mississippi bear hunter and a superb specimen of manhood, was color sergeant of the Twenty-first and a member of Brandon's company. He was tall and straight, broad-shouldered and deep-chested, had an eye like an eagle and a voice like a bull of Bashan, and was full of pluck and power as a panther. He was rough as a bear in manner, but withal a noble, tenderhearted fellow, and a splendid soldier.

The enemy, finding the way now clear, were coming up the street, full company front, with flags flying and bands playing, while the great shells from the siege guns were bursting over their heads and dashing their hurtling fragments after our retreating skirmishers.

Buck was behind the corner of a house taking sight for a last shot. Just as his fingers trembled on the trigger a little three-year-old, fair-haired, baby girl toddled out of an alley, accompanied by a Newfoundland dog, and gave chase to a big shell that was rolling lazily along the pavement, she clapping her little hands and the dog snapping and barking furiously at the shell.

Buck's hand dropped from the trigger. He dashed it across his eyes to dispel the mist and make sure he hadn't passed over the river and wasn't seeing his own baby girl in a vision. No, there is the baby, amid the hell of shot and shell, and here come the enemy. A moment and he has ground his gun, dashed out into the storm, swept his great right arm around the baby, gained cover again, and, baby clasped to his breast and musket trailed in his left hand, is trotting after the boys up to Marye's Heights.

And there behind that historic stone wall and in the lines hard by all those hours and days of terror was that baby kept, her fierce nurses [the soldiers] taking turns patting her while the storm of battle raged and shrieked, and at night wrestling with each other for the boon and benediction of her quiet breathing under their blankets. Never was baby so cared for. They scoured the country-side for milk, and conjured up their best skill to prepare dainty viands for her little ladyship.

When the struggle was over and the enemy had withdrawn to his strongholds across the river, and Barksdale was ordered to reoccupy the town, the Twenty-first Mississippi, having held the post of danger in the rear, was given the place of honor in the van and led the column. There was a long halt, the brigade and regimental staff hurrying to and fro. The regimental colors could not be found.

Denman stood about the middle of the regiment, baby in arms. Suddenly he sprang to the front. Swinging her aloft above his head, her little garments fluttering like the folds of a banner, he shouted, "Forward, Twenty-first, here are your colors!" and without further order off started the brigade toward the town, yelling as only Barksdale's men could yell. They were passing through a street fearfully shattered by the enemy's fire and were shouting their very souls out—but let Buck himself describe the last scene in the drama:

"I was holding the baby high, Adjutant, with both arms, when above all the racket I heard a woman's scream. The next thing I knew I was covered with calico and she fainted on my breast. I caught her before she fell, and laying her down gently, put her baby on her bosom. She was most the prettiest thing I ever looked at, and her eyes were shut;—and—hope God'll forgive me, but I kissed her just once."

The Lone Woman

[Poet Alfred Lord] Tennyson is in error when he says in "Locksley Hall" that "Woman is the lesser man." She is a greater man. A good woman is better than a good man, a bad woman is worse; a brave woman is braver than any man ever was. During the bombardment I was sent into Fredericksburg with a message for General Barksdale. As I was riding down the street that led to his headquarters it appeared to be so fearfully swept by artillery fire that I started to ride across it, with a view of finding some safer way of getting to my destination, when, happening to glance beyond that point, I saw walking quietly and unconcernedly along the same street I was on, and approaching General Barksdale's headquarters from the opposite direction, a lone woman. She apparently found the projectiles which were screaming and exploding in the air, and striking and crashing through the houses, and tearing up the streets, very interesting—stepping a little aside to inspect a great, gaping hole one had just gouged out in the sidewalk, then turning her head to note a fearful explosion in the air. I felt as if it really would not do to avoid a fire which was merely interesting and not at all appalling to a woman, so I stiffened my spinal column as well as I could and rode straight down the street toward headquarters and the self-possessed lady; and having reached the house I rode around back of it to put my horse where he would at least be safer than in front. As I returned on foot to the front the lady had gone up on the porch and was knocking at the door. One of the staff came to hearken, and on seeing a lady, held up his hands, exclaiming in amazement: "What on earth, madam, are you doing here? Do go to some safe place if you can find one." She smiled and said, with some little tartness: "Young gentleman, you seem to be a little excited. Won't you please say to General Barksdale that a lady at the door wishes to see him." The young man assured her General Barksdale could not possibly see her just now; but she persisted. "General Barksdale is a Southern gentleman, sir, and will not refuse to see a lady who has called upon him." Seeing that he could not otherwise get rid of her, the General did come to the door, but actually wringing his hands in excitement and annoyance. "For God's sake, madam, go and seek some place of safety. I'll send a member of my staff to help you find one." She again smiled gently,—while old Barksdale fumed and almost swore,—and then she said quietly: "General Barksdale, my cow has just been killed in my stable by a shell. She is very fat and I don't want the Yankees to get her. If you will send some

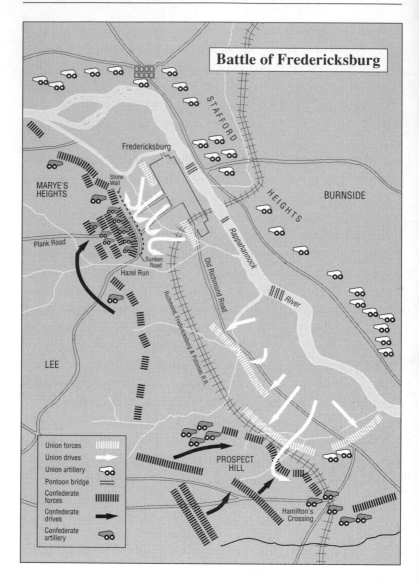

one down to butcher her, you are welcome to the meat."

Years afterwards I delivered a Confederate memorial address at Fredericksburg, and when I told this incident noticed increasing interest and something very like amusement
among the audience, who had ceased to look at me, but all
eyes were turned in one direction; and just as I finished the
story and my eyes followed theirs—there before me sat this

very lady, apparently not a day older, and the entire audience rose and gave her three deafening cheers. . . .

"Up There, You Coward!"

We were stationed on what was afterwards known as "Lee's Hill," an elevation centrally located between the right and left flanks of our line and jutting out at quite a commanding height into and above the plain. For these reasons General Lee made it for the most part his field headquarters during the fight. Portions of the city and of Marye's Heights were not visible, at least not thoroughly so; but every other part of the field was, clear away down, or nearly down, to Hamilton's Crossing. From it we witnessed the break in our lines on the right, where the Federals came in over a piece of marshy ground, supposed to be impassable, between Lane's North Carolina and Archer's Tennessee brigade. The entire attack, from its inception to its unexpected success, was as clearly defined as a movement on a chessboard, and I confess that tears started to and even [fell] from my eyes, but a moment later a great outburst of fire a little back of the line of battle indicated that the intruders had been gallantly met by our second line, or our reserves, and in a few moments out they rushed, the victors yelling at their heels. My uncle, William Henry Stiles, colonel of the Sixtieth Georgia, and who, in the absence of the general, was in command of Lawton's brigade in the battle, told me an amusing story of this particular fight.

When his brigade, with others, was ordered to stem this irruption, drive out the intruders and re-establish—or rather, for the first time properly extend and connect—our lines, his men were double-quicking [rapidly marching] to the point of peril and he running from one end to the other of his brigade line to see that all parts were kept properly "dressed up," when he observed one of the conscripts who had lately been sent to his regiment, a large, fine-looking fellow, drop out and crouch behind a tree. My uncle, a tall, wiry, muscular man, was accustomed to carry a long, heavy sword, and having it at the time in his hand, as he passed he

struck the fellow a sound whack across his shoulders with
the flat of the weapon, simultaneously saying, "Up there,
you coward!" To his astonishment the man dropped his musket, clasped his hands and keeled over backwards, devoutly
ejaculating, "Lord, receive my spirit!"

Uncle William said the entire *dénouement* was so unexpected and grotesque, and his haste so imperative, that he
scarcely knew how he managed to do it, but he did turn and
deliver a violent kick upon the fellow's ribs, at the same
time shouting, "Get up, sir! the Lord wouldn't receive the
spirit of such an infernal coward;" whereupon, to his further
amazement, the man sprang up in the most joyful fashion,
fairly shouting, "Ain't I killed? The Lord be praised!" and
grabbing his musket he sailed in like a hero, as he ever afterwards was. The narrator added that he firmly believed
that but for the kick his conscript would have completed the
thing and died in good order.

*Even in the cold of winter, the Confederate army fought bravely at the Battle of
Fredericksburg.*

On our part of the line I witnessed a scene not quite so hu-
morous as this, but strongly characteristic. I saw a tall Tex-
an bring up the hill, as prisoners, some fifteen or twenty low,
stolid Germans,—Bavarians, I think they were,—no one of

whom could speak a word of English. He must have been a foot taller than any of them, as he stood leaning on his long rifle and looking down upon them with a very peculiar expression. I asked him where he got them and he replied in the most matter-of-fact way, "Well, me and my comrade surrounded 'em; but he got killed, poor fellow!" He really looked as if he could have surrounded the entire lot alone.

A Faithful Servant

Not often have I come in contact with relations more beautiful than existed in some cases between young Southern masters in the service and their slave attendants. These latter belonged for the most part to one of two classes: either they were mature and faithful men, to whose care the lad's parents had committed him, or else they were the special chums and playmates of their young master's boyhood days, and had perhaps already attended and waited upon him in college.

My first cousin, eldest son of the uncle above mentioned, and who was a captain in his regiment, was seriously wounded late in the evening of the battle, but the casualty was not generally known, probably because the surgeons finding him on the field, after a hurried examination, pronounced his wound necessarily and speedily mortal, and added: "We are sorry to leave you, Captain, but we and the litter bearers have all we can attend to." To which he replied: "Certainly, gentlemen, go on and attend to the men; but you are mistaken about me. I haven't the least idea of dying."

They left him; the litter bearers of course did not report his case, and probably neither his father nor any member of his company was aware of his having been wounded. But there was one faithful soul to whom the captain was more than all the rest of the regiment. If he continued "missing" the world was empty to this faithful one, and so, in cold and darkness and sadness, he searched every foot of ground the regiment had fought over, till at last my cousin was found. Then his attendant wandered about until he got from the bodies of dead men blankets enough to make a soft, warm bed, and carefully lifted the wounded man on to it, and covered him snugly. The "boy" then managed to start a fire and get water, and finally, most important of all, got from the body of a dead Federal officer a small flask of brandy and stimulated the captain carefully.

About daylight the doctors came by again and surprised to find him alive, made a more careful examination and found that the ball had passed entirely through his body from right to left, just between the upper and lower vital regions; but they added that he would have died of cold and exposure had it not been for the faithful love that refused to be satisfied until it had found and provided for him. That was the night of the 13th of December. On the 25th, I think it was, he walked up to the third story of a house in Richmond to see my mother, who had meantime gotten through from the North.

The battle closed, as it began, with a marked, and this time a beautiful, natural phenomenon. It was very cold and very clear, and the aurora borealis of the night of December 13th, 1862, surpassed in splendor any like exhibition I ever saw. Of course we enthusiastic young fellows felt that the heavens were hanging out banners and streamers and setting off fireworks in honor of our victory.

Our friends, the enemy, seemed in no hurry to leave our neighborhood, though they did not seem to long for another close grapple, and as we appeared equally indifferent to any closer acquaintance with them, General Burnside and his army on the night of December 15th, apparently insulted, retired to their own side of the river and began to get ready for Christmas.

Chapter 3

Service in the Confederate Army

Chapter Preface

Soon after the start of the Civil War, officers and soldiers on both sides discovered that they were fighting a type of war they had not anticipated. Trained at the army's West Point academy in the military tactics of an earlier time, Confederate commanders had to adapt to drastically different conditions after Fort Sumter and Bull Run. Rough, forested terrain made coordinated movements among large numbers of regiments difficult, sometimes impossible. Longer-range, more accurate rifles took a deadly toll on frontline troops, who began digging entrenchments to protect themselves. Rapid transportation via railroad allowed the enemy to resupply its units. Sniping and guerrilla fighting had to be carried out and defended against. Free-ranging cavalry units played havoc in the rear, disrupting communications and infantry movements.

The skill and pluck of Confederate soldiers carried them to victory in several battles in which they were outnumbered and outmaneuvered. But for the ordinary Confederate soldier, the most common battlefield experience was sheer confusion, as garbled orders and disoriented officers directed them to and fro across the smoke-shrouded battlefields. Added to the terrors of battle were hunger, sickness, the discomforts of camp life, anxiety for distant families, and, eventually, disillusionment and discouragement as the war dragged on for months and years.

Signed up for the duration of the war, thousands of Southerners took advantage of the growing chaos to declare their personal truce with the Union, and by 1864 the greatest enemy faced by the Confederate army was desertion.

Cavalry Service

William G. Stevenson

After a boyhood in Kentucky, William G. Stevenson moved to New York and then to Arkansas, where he entered into a business partnership with George Davis, a gentleman from Memphis. His heart and opinions still largely with the abolitionists and the North, Stevenson found himself surrounded by Southern firebrands, ready at the drop of a hat to fight and die for the right of their region to live and work as it always had. One April morning in 1861, at the outbreak of the Civil War, Stevenson found himself forcefully persuaded to join the Confederate army.

He described his wartime experience in *Thirteen Months in the Rebel Army,* a book published by the New York firm of A.S. Barnes in 1862. Stevenson's account—part memoir, part propaganda—was intended to shock and move the Northern public into throwing itself wholeheartedly into the war effort, to "stir the North," as Stevenson said, "to a profounder sense of the desperate and deadly struggle in which they are engaged than they have ever yet felt." In this the book succeeded—it became a best-seller in New York and other northern cities just as the war turned serious and the brief skirmishes of the early months turned into the huge and desperate battles of late 1862 and 1863.

W hile at Nashville, recovering from the typhoid pneumonia, I resolved to seek a transfer to the cavalry service, as affording me a new field of observation, and perhaps a more stirring and exciting life. As Captin F——s was re-

Excerpted from *Thirteen Months in the Rebel Army*, by William G. Stevenson (New York: A.S. Barnes, 1862).

cruiting a company in and around Nashville, I rode with him from day to day over the country, and thus secured his advocacy of my wishes. On the 4th of February, 1862, I was transferred to his company, and entered it as orderly sergeant, and a vacancy soon occurring, I was promoted to a lieutenancy. Our company was to have been attached to a battalion commanded by Major Howard of Maryland, formerly of the United States army, and as my captain was in service on General Hardee's staff, I acted as captain during the whole of my term in this branch of the service. Shortly after, my company was attached to the command of that celebrated guerrilla leader, Captain J.H. Morgan, at that time, however, acting under the rules of regular warfare, and not, as now, in the capacity of a highway robber.

The system of guerrilla warfare has been endorsed [sanctioned] by an act of the Confederate Congress, and is fully inaugurated over a large part of the South. As there practiced now, it is distinguished from regular warfare by two things: First, the troops are not under any brigade commander, but operate in small bands, much at their pleasure, with a general responsibility to the major-general commanding in their department.

One result of this feature of the system is to develop a large amount of talent in the ranks, as every man has an individual responsibility, and constant opportunities to test his shrewdness and daring. It also gives a perfect knowledge of all roads and localities to the whole force in a given section, as some one or more soldiers will be found in each gang, who, in their frequent maraudings, have traversed every bypath and marked every important point.

Highway Robbery

The second prominent characteristic of guerrilla warfare, is the license it gives to take by force from supposed enemies or neutrals, horses, cash, munitions of war, and, in short, any thing which can aid the party for which he fights; *with the promise of full pay for whatever he brings off to his headquarters*. This is the essential principle of the system, giving it its power and destructiveness. As it displaces patriotism from the breast of the fighter, and substitutes in its room the desire for plunder, the men thus engaged become highway robbers in organized and authorized bands. Nor do guerrilla bands long confine their depredations to known enemies. Wherever a good horse can be found, whatever silver plate is supposed to be secreted, whatever money might be expected, there they concentrate and rob without inquiry as to the character of the owner. Hence the system is destructive to all confidence, and to the safety of even innocent and defenseless females.

It requires no prophet's ken to foresee that the Confederate authorities have commenced a system which will utterly demoralize all engaged in it; destroy the peace, and endanger the safety of non-combatants, and eventually reduce to ruin and anarchy the whole community over which these bands of robbers have their range. . . .

Captain Morgan's Reputation

Morgan, as a citizen in times of peace, maintained the reputation of a generous, genial, jolly, horse-loving, and horse-racing Kentuckian. He went into the Rebellion *con amore* [with love], and pursues it with high enjoyment. He is about thirty-five years of age, six feet in height, well made for strength and agility, and is perfectly master of himself; has a light complexion, sandy hair, and generally wears a mustache, and a little beard on his chin. His eyes are keen, bluish gray in color, and when at rest, have a sleepy look, but he sees every one and everything around him, although apparently unobservant. He is an admirable horseman, and a good shot. As a leader of a battalion of cavalry, he has no superior in the Rebel ranks. His command of his men is supreme. While they admire his generosity and manliness, sharing with them all the hardships of the field, they fear his more than Napoleonic severity for any departure from enjoined duty. His men narrate of him this—that upon one occasion, when engaging in a battle, he directed one of his troopers to perform a hazardous mission in the face of the enemy. The

man did not move. Morgan asked, in short quick words,
"Do you understand my orders?"

"Yes, captain, but I can not obey."

"Then, good-by," said Morgan, and in a moment the cavalryman fell dead from his saddle. Turning to his men, he added, "Such be the fate of every man disobeying orders in the face of an enemy."

No man ever hesitated after that to obey any command.

But Morgan is not without generosity to a foe. A Federal cavalryman related to me, since my escape, an unusual act for an enemy. Losing the command of his wounded horse, which goaded by pain plunged wildly on, he was borne into the midst of Morgan's force. "Don't shoot him!" cried Morgan to a dozen of his men who raised their pistols. "Give him a chance for his life." The pistols were lowered and the man sent back to his own lines unharmed. Few men have appeared on either side in this contest who combine dash and caution, intrepidity and calmness, boldness of plan with self-possession in execution, as does Morgan. The feat reported of him in Nashville, shortly after the Rebel army retreated through it, illustrates this. Coming into the city full of Federal soldiers in the garb of a farmer with a load of meal, he generously gives it to the commissary department, saying, in an undertone, that there are some Union men out where he lives, but they have to be careful to dodge the Rebel cavalry, and he wishes to show his love for the cause by this little donation. Going to the St. Cloud to dine, he sits at the same table with General McCook, since cruelly murdered, and is pointed out to the Federal officer as the Union man who had made the generous gift. He is persuaded to take the value of it in gold, and then, in a private interview, tells the Federal officer that a band of Morgan's cavalry is camping near him, and if one or two hundred cavalry will come down there to-morrow he will show them how to take Morgan. The cavalry go, and *are taken* by Morgan. So the story goes. An equally successful feat it was, to step into the telegraph office in Gallatin, Tennessee, at a later date, as he did, dressed as a Federal officer, and there learn from the operator the time when the down-train would be in, and arrest it, securing many thousands of dollars without loss of men or time. Another anecdote of his cool daring and recklessness is this. Riding up to a picket post near Nashville, dressed in full Federal uniform, he sharply reproved the sentinel on duty for not calling out the guard to salute the officer of the day, as he announced himself to be. The sentinel stammered out, as an excuse, that he did not know him to be the officer of the day. Morgan ordered him to give up his arms, because of this breach of duty, and the man obeyed. He then called out the remaining six men of the guard, including the lieutenant who was in charge, and put them under arrest, ordering them to pile their arms, which they did. He then marched them down the road a short distance where his own men were concealed, and secured all of them, and their arms and horses, without resistance.

In an engagement Morgan is perfectly cool, and yet his face and action are as if surcharged with electricity. He has the quickness of a tiger, and the strength of two ordinary men. One cause of his success is found in the character of his chargers. He has only the fleetest and most enduring horses; and when one fails he soon finds another by hook or by crook. His business in his recent raid into Kentucky (July 29th), seemed to have been mainly to gather up the best blooded horses, in which that State abounds.

Unless in some fortunate hour for the loyal cause he should fall into the hands of the Federal forces, Colonel John H. Morgan will become one of the most potent and dangerous men in the Rebel service.

Cavalry Tactics

So far as my observation extended, the Southern cavalry are superior to the loyal [Union], for the kind of service expected of them. They are not relied upon for heavy charges against large bodies of infantry closely massed, as in some of the wars of the Old World during the close of the last century and the first part of this; but for scouting, foraging, and sudden dashes against outposts and unguarded companies of their enemies. In this service, fleetness, perfect docility, and endurance for a few hours a day, are requisite in the make-up of the horses used. And in these traits Morgan's blooded horses are admirable. And then, with the exception of some of the Western troopers, the Southerners are more perfect horsemen than our loyal cavalry. They have been on horseback, many of them, from youth, and are trained to the perfect control of themselves and their steeds in difficult circumstances. In addition to these causes of superiority, they have a vast advantage over the Federal troops in the present contest from two causes: It is hard to overestimate the advantage they find in a knowledge of the ground, the roads, the ravines, the hiding-places, the marshes, the fords, the forests, &c. But even more important than this is the sympathy they have from the inhabitants, almost universally, who give them information by every method, of the approach, strength, and plans of their enemies. Even the negroes will be found often, either from fear or other motives, to give all the information they can obtain to the Southerners. And the Southerners know far better than we do how to obtain, and sift, and estimate, the value of what the slaves tell them.

From these causes, we should look for and expect no little trouble from the mounted men, who will continue to constitute a pretty large element in the Rebel forces.

Panic in Nashville

After commencing my service in the cavalry, we spent some three weeks in scouting and foraging, having Nashville for our center. During this time I rode as courier several times, on one occasion riding sixty miles, from Nashville to Shelbyville, in seven hours. Upon another occasion, my blooded horse made fourteen miles in a little less than fifty minutes; but this was harder service than we generally exacted from our horses. Upon reporting myself to General Breckenridge, for whom this arduous service had been performed, he merely said *"Très bien"*[very well]—from which I saw that he expected prompt work from those who served him.

On Saturday the 15th of February, the report came that General Johnson would evacuate Bowling Green, and Sunday morning we learned, to the amazement of citizens and soldiers, that Fort Donelson was taken [by Union forces under General Ulysses Grant]. Never was there greater commotion than Nashville exhibited that Sabbath morning. Churches were closed, Sabbath schools failed to assemble, citizens gathered in groups, consulted hastily, and then rushed to their homes to carry out their plans. Bank directors were speedily in council, and Confederate officials were everywhere engrossed in the plan of evacuation. A general stampede commenced. Specie [money] was sent off to Columbia and Chattanooga, plate was removed, and valuables huddled promiscuously into all kinds of vehicles. Hack-hire rose to twenty-five dollars an hour, and personal service to fabulous prices. Government property was removed as fast as transportation could be furnished. Vast amounts of provisions and ammunition had been accumulated at Nashville, for the armies at Donelson and Bowling Green; and so confident were they of holding those points, that no provision had been made for retreat. . . .

My company was constantly on scout duty, guarding the roads on the north side of the [Cumberland] river, protecting the rear of the retreating hosts, and watching for the coming of [Union General Augustus] Buell's advance. This whole retreat, from Bowling Green to Corinth, a distance of nearly three hundred miles as traveled by the army, and occupying six weeks, was one of the most trying that an army was ever called upon to perform in its own country and among friends. The army was not far from 60,000 strong, after General George B. Crittenden's forces were added to it at Murfreesboro. The season of the year was the worst possible in that latitude. Rain fell, sometimes sleet, four days out of seven. The roads were bad enough at best, but under such a tramping of horses and cutting of wheels as the march produced, soon became horrible. About a hundred regiments were numbered in the army. The full complement of wagons to each regiment—twenty-four—would give above two thousand wagons. Imagine such a train of heavily loaded wagons, passing along a single mud road, accompanied by 55,000 infantry and 5000 horsemen, in the midst of rain and sleet, day after day, camping at night in wet fields or dripping woods, without sufficient food adapted to their wants, and often without any tents, the men lying down in their wet clothes, and rising chilled through and through; and let this continue for six weeks of incessant retreat, and you get a feeble glimpse of what we endured. The army suffered great loss from sickness and some from desertion; some regiments leaving Bowling Green with six or seven hundred men, and reaching Corinth with but half of this number. The towns through which we passed were left full of sick men, and many were sent off to hospitals at some distance from our route.

One of the most desperate marches men were ever called to encounter, was performed by General Breckenridge's division between Fayetteville and Huntsville. They moved at ten A.M., and marched till one o'clock next morning, making thirty miles over a terrible road, amid driving rain and sleet during the whole time. The reason for this desperate work was, that a day's march lay between the rear-guard and the main body of General Johnson's army, and there was danger that it would be cut off. It cost the general hundreds of men. One-fourth of the division dropped out of the ranks unable to proceed, and were taken up by the guard, until every wagon and ambulance was loaded, and then scores were deserted on the road, who straggled in on following days, or made their way back to their homes in Tennessee or Kentucky.

This retreat left a good deal of desolation in its track; for although the officers endeavored to restrain their men, yet they must have wood; and where the forest was sometimes a mile from the camping ground, and fences were near, the fences suffered; and where sheep and hogs abounded when we came, bones and bristles were more abundant after we left. Horses were needed in the army; and after it left, none were seen on the farms. And then the impressed soldiers [civilians forced to serve], judging from my own feelings, were not over-scrupulous in guarding the property of Rebels. The proud old planters, who had aided in bringing on the rebellion, were unwillingly compelled to bear part of its burdens. . . .

Chasing Down Friendlies

A ludicrous scene occurred at this time, illustrating the liability to panic to which even brave men are sometimes subject. While resting at Murfreesboro, of course we were liable to be overtaken by Buell's cavalry, and as Colonel Morgan was not a man to be caught asleep, he kept scouting parties ever on the alert, scouring the country on different roads for miles in the direction of the Federal army. I was in command of a squad of eight men, with whom I made a long and rapid march in the direction of Lebanon, and when returning by a different route, night overtook us some fifteen miles from camp. After getting supper at a farm-house, we were again in the saddle at ten o'clock of a calm, quiet evening, with a dim moon to light us back to camp. We jogged on unsuspicious of danger, as we were now on the return from the direction of the Federal cavalry. Within ten miles of camp, near midnight, we passed through a lane and were just entering a forest, when we became aware that a cavalry force was approaching on the same road; but who they were, or how many, we had no idea. We were not expecting another party of our men in this direction, and yet they could hardly be Federals, or we would have heard of them, as we had been near their lines, and among the friends of the Southern cause.

Acting on the principle that it is safer to ask than to answer questions in such circumstances, I instantly ordered them to "Halt," and asked, "Who comes there?" Their commander was equally non-committal, and demanded, "Who comes there?"

"If you are friends, advance and give the countersign," said I; but scarcely was the word uttered when the buckshot from the shot-guns of the head of the column came whistling past us in dangerous but not fatal proximity. Thus challenged, I instantly ordered, "Draw saber— Charge!" and with a wild yell we dashed at them, determined to keep our course toward our camp, whoever they might be. To our surprise, they broke and ran in disorder, and we after them, yelling with all the voice we could command. I soon saw, from their mode of riding and glimpses of their dress, that they were Confederates; but as we had routed them, though seven times our number,— there were sixty-five of them,—we determined to give them a race. Keeping my men together, yelling in unison, and firing in the air occasionally, we pressed them closely six or seven miles. When within three miles of camp, I drew my men up and told them we must get in by another route, and, if possible, as soon as they. A rapid ride by a longer road brought us to the lines in a few minutes, and we found the whole force of over a thousand cavalrymen mounting to repel an attack from a formidable force of Federal cavalry, which had driven in the scouting party of sixty-five men, after a desperate encounter. I immediately reported the whole affair to Morgan, when, with a spice of humor which never forsakes him, he told me to keep quiet; and, calling up the lieutenant who was in charge of the scouting party, ordered him to narrate the whole affair. The lieutenant could not say how many Federal cavalry there were, but there must have been from three to five hundred, from the rattling of sabers and the volume of sound embodied in their unearthly yells. At all events, their charge was terrific, and his wonder was that any of his men escaped. How many of the Federals had fallen it was impossible to estimate, but some were seen to fall, &c.

When Morgan had learned the whole story, with the embellishments, he dismissed the lieutenant. But the story was too good to keep, and by morning the scare and its cause were fully ventilated, greatly to the chagrin of Major Bennett's battalion, to which the routed men belonged. They were questioned daily about "those three hundred Yankees who made that terrific charge;" and whenever a loud noise of any kind was made, even by a mule, it was asked, with a serious face, if that was equal to "the unearthy yells of the Yankees." Indeed, for weeks, "the three hundred Yankees" was a by-word of ridicule, in reply to any boast from one of Bennett's men.

Camping with the Ninth Louisiana

Reuben Allen Pierson

In many places, the Confederate cause commanded service from entire families. Reuben Allen Pierson, from Bienville Parish in northern Louisiana, was one of four Pierson brothers who served the Southern cause. He was first mustered into Company C, Ninth Louisiana Infantry, on July 7, 1861, and by the end of the year was promoted to the rank of sergeant. He re-enlisted on February 5, 1862, while serving in Virginia and three months later became a regimental captain—less than a year after joining the Confederate army as a lowly private.

In 1862, Pierson's Ninth Louisiana participated in the Shenandoah Valley campaign, in which General Stonewall Jackson led a brilliant chase of several Union armies through the hills and valleys of northwestern Virginia. The regiment later earned a good reputation through several important battles, including the Seven Days' Battles near Richmond. At the Battle of Second Manassas, the regiment suffered heavy casualties and eventually ran out of ammunition, after which its enlisted men took up stones to fight off an assault by Union troops.

In late 1861, the Ninth Louisiana prepared to go into its first winter quarters (Civil War campaigns generally came to a halt late in the year and then resumed in the spring). In the war's off-season, the concern of the ordinary soldier, as Pierson's letters home to his father reveal, turned from fighting and marching to bad food, sickness, discomfort, and boredom.

Excerpted from the wartime letters of Reuben Allen Pierson (1861) as reprinted in *Brothers in Gray*, edited by Thomas W. Cutrer and T. Michael Parrish (Baton Rouge: Louisiana State University Press, 1997).

Camp Florida, Va.
Novr. 26th, 1861

D ear Father
It has been only a few days since I wrote [brother] James a letter and send it by Mr. Poole, but having another opportunity to send one by old [Sergeant Major] A.P. King who has been discharged from service on account of feeble health, I will write you a short letter. I am now enjoying excellent health—never felt heartier in all my life. The health of our company is only tolerable. Smith Scogin is the only bad case we have. He has pneumonia very bad; all the Lebanon boys are in good health. Collins is still in Culpepper hospital, and I suppose or at least have heard is taking the dropsy. I intend going to see him in a few days if I can get off. We expect to be sent into winter quarters in a few days. The weather is very cold. We had a light snow a few nights back which is still lying on the ground in some places. I have an abundance of clothes to last me till spring, and intend to take every precaution to make myself healthy.

We are now encamped in the midst of a large army where we can neither see or hear anything except the roar of the cannon or military preparations. We cannot buy anything at price so we live on the rations drawn from the com[m]issary which is very good, plenty of fat beef, and enough bacon for about 2 days in every week—we also draw a small ration of sugar & coffee enough for to make a cupful per day to each man. As for breadstuffs we have more than we use a portion of which is cornmeal. We marched out on review yesterday where I saw (for the first time) the whole La. brigade together. It was quite a brilliant scene. On every side as far as the eye coul[d] view might be seen the glistening bayonets of troops and the flying colors of each regimental flag as they marched some to and some from the grand review. But the most exquisite part of all was the commingled sound of about thirty excellent brass bands as they echoed from hilltop to hilltop. It seemed indeed as if it was a world of music. I saw [Confederate] General [Kirby] Smith who looks as plain as some old farmer, but his keen eye and flashing countenance told of the sparkling intellect which lay hidden within. We received a telegraphic dispatch here this morning that [Confederate] Gen. [Braxton] Bragg had succeeded in taking Fort Pickens [in Pensacola Harbor, Florida]. I hope it may prove true and that many other victories of the same kind may follow till Old Abe [Lincoln] and all his cabinet become convinced that a supreme being is sending a just punishment upon them for their wickedness in waging war upon an unoffending country who plead for justice and right. I am ever proud to receive the compliments of the young ladies and therefore must request that you give my best regards to all the ladies of our peaceful village, and especially to Miss Belle from whom I have received many tokens of true friendship. She is one of those who seldom forgets an old friend. Tell her Peter [the Pierson family's slave] is well and merry as a lark in spring. Give my respects to all old friends. Receive the same yourself and family. Give my love to Mr. & Mrs. Randle. Tell Mrs. R that nothing could have renewed in my mind the happy days spent while boarding with her so quick[ly] as the delicious bottle of wine which she sent me. It was indeed a treat. I must also return my thanks to a loved Father for the quart of old bourbon. It was the best spirits I have met with since I left home. Excuse all amiss and pardon any blunder and attribute it to haste.

I remain your affectionate Son

Camp Florida, Va.
Decr. 3rd, 1861

Dear Father

I received your late favor sent by [Lieutenant James] Egan [a physician with Pierson's company] last night and was exceedingly glad to hear from you and the family. My health is still good and I think with proper care I may come out through the remainder of our time without a single day['']s sickness. I am acting as orderly (our first sergeant being absent at Richmond sick). This excuses me from guard duty.

There is nothing of importance going on here now—now and then a little skirmish between the pickets. We have not been sent into winter quarters yet though we have been expecting an order to that effect for more than a month. We will go out on picket duty in a few days which will be my first trip. The Regt. has only been once and that was while I was sick. When I return I will give you the particulars of the tour. The weather is exceedingly cold to us up here—water freezes in a few moments after it is brought from the spring and the wind is blowing continually. You wrote to me to state in my next letter whether I had received my bundle of goods or not. I have received them all and also the $25.00 sent by Mr. Candler. I have as many clothing as could do me any service through winter. I have a splendid overcoat which cost me in a trading way ($5.75) five dollars and six bits. I have as much money as I want and will have more than I started with when we draw. The government will soon be indebted to us for four months, which will amount to over sixty dollars.

The general health of the regiment is still bad. Several have died in the last few weeks and others are now quite sick. Smith Scogin is at Manassas very low, and John Evans, son of Hiram Evans was very sick at Richmond when I heard from there last. Collins is still at Culpepper Court House in bad health, but able to walk over town. I fear his health is permanently injured. The Key boys are complaining with cold though nothing serious. George Whitley is also a little unwell. Tom Pittman, Horace Rhodes, Lamar, Charles Prothro, Aaron Wells, Frank Harrison, the Colbert boys and Prentiss Jackson are all as full of life and merriment as a drove of young mules. In fact all our company are in an improving way with but few exceptions. There is much rejoicing in camps on account of the return of our Surgeon. Most of the boys seem to think their lives are dependent on him. They flock around him as thick as bees flock to their king. Tell Jim I received his letter sent by Egan and will answer it in a few days. Tell Aunt Nan & Joe they must write to me in cahoots. I would like to hear from them. Give my love to all old friends especially Mr. Randle[']s family who seem like relatives when I think of the kind treatment shown me while boarding there. Excuse all amiss and attribute it to haste. I send this by Uncle Robert Burnett who leaves here this evening. Receive the warmest affections (yourself and all the family) of a dutiful Son.

At Camp near Manassas, Va. Decr. 22nd, 1861

Dear Father

I received yours dated the 11th Inst. [of this month] in nine days and have neglected to write till now on account of my having written a letter to Jim the day I received yours. We are in our position for the winter and quite busily engaged in building huts to shield us from the severity of this climate. We have had a fine fall; the weather has been more favorable than any of us ever anticipated. It seems that the God who rules the seasons, as well as the destinies of nations has seen fit to smile upon us and protect us from the many diseases to which we are subject in exchanging our mild southern clime for the mountainous region of the Old Dominion [Virginia]. It is true that we have suffered considerable by colds contracted from lying upon the cold damp ground under a tent made of cloth, through which the piercing winds could easily pass. I am still in fine health. Whenever I feel the least symptoms of sickness I resort to the old remedy (Moffats Pills) which restores me to health and prevents disease. I have but little news to write. Frank Long died at Richmond a few days ago. The health of our company is still bad. There are 13 privates and two non-commissioned officers back at hospitals, and 12 privates reported sick in camp this morning with one noncommissioned officer, making the total sick in our company 28 while we only have 39 men for duty in camps. We have 7 men on extra or daily duty and two on detached service, also four non-commissioned officers in camp for duty making a total of 80 men not including [the] commissioned officers. Notwithstanding all this sick[ness, optimism] prevails, having lost three men in less than one month, still some say the health is tolerable good. I only make this statement that you and all others, who desire may know how things stand with us. Some

Desertion

Desertion became a sore temptation for soldiers struggling with sickness, hunger, fatigue, boredom, danger, and the sense of futility that grew worse as the war dragged on. Some resisted temptation; others could not. In many cases, the pleas of one's family became the deciding factor, as James M. McPherson explains in For Cause and Comrades: Why Men Fought in the Civil War.

Desertion rates were probably higher among married than unmarried soldiers, especially in the Confederacy where Union invasions and food shortages threatened soldiers' families with danger and hunger. A good many Confederate soldiers deserted in response to such letters from their wives as this one from Alabama in 1864: "We haven't got nothing in the house to eat but a little bit o meal. . . . If you put off a-coming, 'twont be no use to come, for we'll all hands of us be out there in the grave yard with your ma and mine."

But there were married privates with a sense of duty and honor as highly developed as any officer's. "I came to the war because I felt it to be my duty," wrote a private in the 18th Georgia in 1863 to his wife, who had told him that his two daughters were pleading for him to come home. "I am not going to run away if I never come home I had rather di without seeing them than for peple to tell them after I am dead that their father was a deserter. . . . It [is] every Southern mans duty to fight against abolition misrule and preserve his Liberty untarnished which was won by our fore Fathers. . . . I never yet regretted the step I have taken." A Tennessee cavalryman who also had two daughters said he "would rather die an honorable Death than to Bring Reproach or Dishonor upon my family or friends."

James M. McPherson, *For Cause and Comrades: Why Men Fought in the Civil War.*
New York: Oxford University Press, 1997.

of this number are staying back at hospitals to shirk out of duty, but very few in our company do this. There was a fight between the federals and our men above here one day this week. I have not learned the full particulars yet though our loss was severe. Times are very dull. Only three days till Christmas and no excitement. Our mess have eggs and sugar enough to make a nog, if we can only procure the spirits to mix with them & we have the promise of getting some. Some of our officers are of opinion that old Abe & his cabinet will have to knock under now as England has demanded [the release of arrested Confederate diplomats John] Slidell and [James] Mason, on the passport of [British Minister] Lord Lyons, so that she may obtain her rights and sustain her flag if it costs a war with the boasted fanatics who pretend to be contending for a great national union. Time can only unravel the hidden mysteries of the future and by waiting we will all see what is next. We received a letter from our Capt a few days since in which he said he would return in the spring or rather in January. He sent many compliments to the boys. Most of us are proud that he will return for we fare better when he is here on account of his influence with the other officers. Some few are down on him but still any man who commands a company will have enemies. I cannot blame him for the turn he took to get his seat, that he might free himself from camp during the winter. A great many of our boys are nearly crazy to get furloughs to go home, but I think they will all fail. Both of the Lieuts are anxious to go but the Capt being absent ties them. You wrote to me in a very feeling manner upon the subject of our being separated and in all probability for life yet your earnest desire and prayer seemed to be that I should prepare myself to meet you once more if it was after death. I can only say that I am yet a wayward and reckless being out of the harbor of safety and nearing the verge of eternity. When I reflect upon these solemn and important thoughts my eyes overflow with tears and my heart aches with the burden of grief. I almost wish that I had perished while yet an infant or never had being. It is the earnest wish of my heart that we may all be spared till another summer when we may be allowed to assemble in a family group and there hold converse with one another. You spoke of hiring out my negroes at the 1st of January. Do as you like with them, for I seldom think anything about what disposition would be best to make with them. They are mine and will be till this war panic shall cease. I owe a considerable sum in the stores at [the Louisiana towns of] Lebanon & Sparta and when I draw pay again I will send you 50 or 60 dollars which you can dispose of as you think proper. Tell my creditors to be easy. I shall not be absent always. The Confederacy is now in debt to us for four months['] service which will amount to some 60 dollars and I have that much owing to me in the company besides a little which I have kept for hard times. Excuse all amiss. Give my regards to all my old friends whom you may see, especially to any of the fair sex as no one esteems women more highly than I. She is the only jewel of earth worth man[']s attention, and she serves as a guiding star to him along the rough journey of life. I am becoming childish which never can please the fancy of a stern man like you. With my most sincere devotion to you and all the family I subscribe myself your affectionate Son though absent.

Swindling and Soldiering

Robert C. Carden

Born in Coffee County, Tennessee, in 1843, Robert C. Carden enlisted in the Confederate army at Manchester, Tennessee, in May 1861. He served in Company B of the 16th Tennessee Infantry Regiment until January 1865. The regiment fought in several crucial battles, including Perryville, Murfreesboro, and Chickamauga, that took place in the Civil War's "Central" theater—that is, within Tennessee, Kentucky, and northern Georgia.

In 1911, Robert Carden traveled to Boone, Iowa, to visit one of his sons. While there, the old veteran met several of his former Union army opponents and was prevailed on to recount his personal story of life in the Confederate army. The stories were collected into a series of articles for Boone's local newspaper, and then found their way into a scrapbook kept by his grandson. Too fragile to copy or scan, the articles were transcribed by hand by Carden's great-grandson, and now appear on the Civil War Virtual Archives website.

Carden's tales reveal that he felt more enthusiasm for cleverly procuring life's necessities—particularly good food and apple brandy—than for fighting and killing Union soldiers, for whom he held a brotherly regard.

We remained in camp for a few days and then marched in a northerly direction, passing through the country where several companies of our regiment were raised and

Excerpted from "Civil War Memories of Robert C. Carden," on the website of the Civil War Virtual Archives, www2.dmci.net.

we could see women and children on the roads to greet their loved ones as we marched along. We arrived at Gainsboro, on the Cumberland river and stopped for a rest. A lot of us went down to the river to go in bathing, and I remember a circumstance that occurred while we were in the river. Some of our teamsters came down to water their mules and one of our boys asked permission of one of the teamsters to lead one of the mules into the water. There were several in the water at the time and the mule soon got into deep water and if there ever was a circus that mule certainly made one. It was but a little while till everybody was out on the bank and the soldier and the mule had the whole river to themselves. The soldier finally got away from the mule and we thought sure the animal would drown. Sometimes his head would come to the surface, then the other end would show up, then his feet were up, then he would disappear altogether, but he finally quit his capers, stuck his nose out of the water, circled around a little and came ashore.

After resting up a few days we started northward toward Kentucky. We passed several towns, that I do not remember much about, after fifty years, but I remember that we passed through Bardstown. We also went out of our way to a place named Munfordsville where about 4,500 Yankees had repulsed some of our cavalry but when they found they had [Confederate General Braxton] Bragg's army before them they surrendered.

I never saw any of them but I remember the night before the surrender we were lying down in the road and by the side of it, when a wagon or artillery got up a big hub-bub and if there ever was a scared lot of tired out Rebels it was us. Everyone was asleep, I suppose, and such running and scrambling I never saw. I remember that I was so scared that I left my gun lying in the road and everybody seemed to be hunting a tree to get behind. I think a Yankee corporal's guard could have captured the whole outfit. I understood at the time that the panic ran through the whole army. I was in another panic in Georgia and it was on the same order. Everybody was scared almost to death and it started in the same way.

Fighting at Perryville

From here we continued our march until we arrived at Perryville, Kentucky. The battle of Perryville was fought on the 8th day of October, 1863. Gen. Bragg said in his report of the battle that his forces did not exceed 40,000, all told, and that [Union] Gen. [Don Carlos] Buell had about two to one. Bragg says: "We captured, wounded and killed not less than 25,000 of the enemy, took over thirty cannon, 17,000 small arms, some 2,000,000 cartridges for the same, destroyed over a hundred wagons and brought out of Kentucky more than a hundred more with mules and harness complete, replaced our horses by a fine mount and lived two months on rations captured from the enemy, and secured material to clothe the army."

I remember we went into the battle close to a small creek. We had just got to the top of a small hill when we saw the enemy rise to their feet and then business began, and things were hot for a time. There was a battery on our left that was giving us grape [grapeshot: canvas-covered fragmentation shells] and canister [small fragmentation shells] and the bullets were singing around us. A man was standing just in front of me while I was loading my gun and I happened to have my eyes on him just as a canister struck him in the breast and I saw the white flesh before it bled. He was a dead man.

Col. John H. Savage, in his report of the engagement said that our regiment, the 16th Tennessee, killed the Yankee general [James] Jackson. The Yankee general was one of the bravest men that ever went into battle. Some of my company was close by him when he was killed. They said that he was standing on some part of a cannon with his hat in his hand, urging his men to put it to us. Our men demanded his surrender but he would not notice a word they said and in the conflict some one shot him dead.

After giving the Yankees a good thrashing we started to hunt some more to whip. We had full possession of the battlefield but our rations being about out we started for Cumberland Gap. On this retreat I suffered more with hunger than I ever did during the war. I remember one day on that march myself and a comrade were sitting down by the road to rest when our Assistant Surgeon came riding by and I asked him if he could give a fellow a bite of something to eat. He reached down in his haversack and gave me a biscuit which I divided with my comrade, and I think to this day how good that biscuit tasted. We had a hard time on this trip as the Yankees had been over this road on their way to Cumberland Gap, and where they had been there wasn't much left for us.

Applejack Escapades

From Cumberland Gap we went to the railroad above Knoxville and took the cars to Tullahoma and went into camp where we stayed for some time. I was then within 14 miles of home and I visited home quite often. Our adjutant liked a drink of applejack [homemade brandy] quite well and as there was a still near my home I would get a pass frequently. I suppose our Colonel did not know anything about it, so I would run up home, visit the folks and lay in a jug of brandy.

I remember on one occasion while we were camped there one of our company had been out about five miles to visit his people and a night or so later four or five of us went out to where this fellow reported that his brother-in-law, a preacher at that, had a lot of liquor on hand and was selling it. As we did not want to buy any, one of the crowd acted as officer, and he told the preacher we wanted some liquor, and as he said he had some the officer told him we would have to take him to camp together with what liquor he had. If you ever heard any begging that preacher did it. As we didn't want the preacher some of us told the officer that if he would promise not to sell any more we would let him off but we would be compelled to take what liquor he had, which we did, and let him go.

As quick as we got started we commenced to store it away and when we got back to camp we were a lively set. It was a cold frosty night and the first thing I did after getting to camp was to try to catch a dog. We had an old fellow in our company who had a little wooly dog. I had a big fish hook and baited it with a piece of meat and proceeded to catch the dog. He did not take hold of it for some time and while I was lying down on my stomach expecting him to bite one of our crowd became boisterous down on the company grounds and an officer was about to put him in the guard house. One of the boys started down there to help him out of the difficulty and I heard him go kersplash into one of the wells we had dug. I was so tickled that I knew the old fellow who owned the dog would hear me laughing so I jumped up to run just as the dog got the bait in his mouth and I dragged him a little distance when the fish hook tore loose and the dog got away. But Charlie Lance got an awful cold bath just the same.

We stayed at Tullahoma for some time until we heard of [Union General William] Rosecrans and a lot of Yankees at Nashville, and as we had whipped Buell at Perryville, we hiked off down to Murfreesboro, passing through Manchester, my home town, so I got permission (I suppose) and went out two miles to see my mother and stayed all night at home, and was back to my command by daylight the next morning.

It took us two days to march to Murfreesboro and we stayed there some time until Rosecrans came out from Nashville to see what we were doing.

We marched out four or five miles on the Nashville road and formed in line of battle and the first thing Mr. Rosecrans knew we were onto him. Our forces put it to him hard and heavy, driving back his right back some distance but we could not move them back but a little where the river turns north from the pike and railroad, so we started south toward Chattanooga to see if we could find some Yankees to whip. . . .

Some Devilment

At Chattanooga we went into camp southeast of town and had a very good time there. As usual, when I didn't have any Yankees to whip I was in some devilment. I had a chum who was always ready for anything and when necessary I would write a pass, sign all the necessary officers' names to it and we would go to town. I had two trusty comrades, Bob Tucker and John Robinson. Robinson and I would go to town and he would borrow $10 off somebody, then we would proceed to enclose the quart. The quart cost $10. Then we would find where some citizen was selling it on the sly. I would take our canteens and go where it was kept for sale, go in and find that he had it, get my vessels full, sit down and have a big talk. About the time we got in a good way Robinson would rush in, the maddest man you ever saw. He would cuss and abuse me, threaten to kick me out of the house, etc., then he would turn to the man and tell him what he would do to me when he got me back to camp, and while that was going on I would quietly walk out with the liquor. They would talk a while (to give me time to get away) then Robinson would say he must go. When the man would say that I had not paid for the whisky, then Robinson was madder than ever. He would cuss and tear around and say he had given me the money to pay for it and he would go and bring me back. He would finally locate me out of town and as our business in town had been transacted we would go back to camp.

On another occasion I took Bob Tucker. Bob had been to town the day before and had partly made a deal for a lot of ginger cakes and had told the fellow he would go back to camp and come in the next day with his partner and close the deal. So I fixed up our credentials and we lit out for town. When we got to the fellow's store, a small concern, he was very busy with customers and told us to walk into the back room, and he would be in soon. He had the cakes in sheets about the size of a door but had a lot cut up into regulation size. About this time we heard an awful noise in the alley and the door being locked I jumped up and caught the transom and held there to see what was the matter and while there Tucker was stuffing my haversack full of cakes. I held on till he filled it and then let loose and as he had his filled we thought while the commotion lasted we would walk out the door. The only thing that had happened was a white fellow had knocked a negro down in the alley. We returned to camp with about as many ginger cakes as anybody ever carried in tow haversacks.

A few days afterwards a fellow came to camp selling pies and other things out of a wagon. I went up to where he was doing business and at once saw he was in need of a clerk, as everything was going like hot cakes. I said: "Mister, you don't seem to be able to wait on them all. I will help you if you want me to." He said, "All right," so I got up in the hind end of the wagon and the way I sold truck was a sight. Robinson, my partner, and messmate wanted a whole lot of stuff and would buy only of me. He would buy 75 cents worth and give me a dollar and I would give him three or four dollars change. Now and then when Robinson was gone I would hand over what money I had to the boss. But Robinson was the best customer we had.

A Woman's Fight

Service to the military was not limited to volunteer nursing for the women of the Confederate and Union armies. Writer Elizabeth Leonard, in All the Daring of the Soldier, *reveals the conditions that allowed females to surreptitiously march and fight with the men and boys.*

Women soldiers who evaded or made it through the physical examination process soon discovered that many of the features of regular Civil War army life also provided effective shields against the discovery of their sex. Army life in the 1860s was significantly different from army life in the late twentieth century. For one thing, recruitment was rarely if ever followed by anything resembling modern-day boot camp with its intensive physical training. Rather, the focus was generally on learning how to drill. Wrote one Pennsylvania soldier after six months in the army: "The first thing in the morning is drill, then drill, then drill again. Then drill, drill, a little more drill. Then drill, and lastly drill. Between drills, we drill and sometimes stop to eat a little and have a roll-call." In new units at least, "drilling" meant learning how to handle, load, and fire guns and how to parry and

In the evening the fellow went to the Colonel and told him he had a load that ought to have brought him $250 or $300 and he only got about $50 out of it. I felt sorry for the fellow and never charged him a cent for helping him. I'm telling these things as few would know of the kind traits of a soldier if I did not.

I was going down Main street in Chattanooga one day when I saw a crowd of soldiers gathered around a big fat fellow, a Colonel of a Tennessee regiment, who was full as a tick. He had a fish pole on his shoulder and seemed to be headed for the river. The boys were teasing him and they got him red hot. He would cuss them with all the cuss words he could muster up and he could muster a whole lot of them. He told them they would desert if they were not so far from

---

thrust with a bayonet, practicing simple maneuvers, and marching. In the early weeks of their military service, women soldiers' efforts, like those of their male comrades, centered on such gender-neutral exercises. Of course, women soldiers also had to learn to carry their own gear, which typically included a gun, a bayonet and scabbard, ammunition, blankets, a canteen, clothing, stationery, photographs, toiletries, and a mending kit, plus equipment for cooking and eating rations. But once they grew accustomed to the forty to fifty pounds of matériel they had to carry, as many men also needed to accustom themselves, women soldiers rarely had to fear that additional biologically based differences in physical strength would lead to their disclosure.

Moreover, camp life, although intimate in some ways, allowed for sufficient freedom of movement to enable women soldiers to avoid notice when bathing and dealing with other personal matters. Civil War soldiers lived and slept in close proximity to one another, but they rarely changed their clothes. Furthermore, they passed the bulk of their time, day and night, out of doors, where they also attended to their bodily needs.

Elizabeth D. Leonard, *All the Daring of the Soldier: Women of the Civil War Armies.* New York: W.W. Norton & Company, 1999.

home and he handed it out to them in fine style. One of the soldiers said, "Well, old man, go on about your fishing. I hope you'll catch lots of fish." He said, "I hope I won't get a d—d bite."

In the Chickamauga Country

While we were camped on Missionary ridge we went up the river a short distance where a creek run into the Tennessee river above Chattanooga and the first we knew a lot of Yankees opened up on us and we got away from there in short order. I remember while we were camped there I took a couple of canteens and went down to a spring to get some water. The spring was in a narrow gulley and I saw three Muscovy ducks about half grown so I spread myself out like a woman spreads her dress when she is driving a hen and chicks; I did that to keep them from going by me. When one came near enough I would grab it, pull its head off and put it in my shirt bosom. I served them all the same way and they cut up and flopped until the front of my shirt was as bloody as though a hog had been butchered in my bosom. But I tell you they were fine eating on an empty stomach.

We camped around Chattanooga until the Yankees came down about the Chickamauga country and concluded to give us a spanking. We were not ready to take it so we ran together and put it to them in fine style. We were going to run them into Chattanooga and I guess we would have done it if it had not been for Thomas. We lost lots of men there and the other side lost heavily too. I drew one minie ball [bullet]. It glanced across my cheek about half an inch from my right eye and the scar is there now. I don't know how many I killed for I had no chance to count them. I was sent to a hospital below there but was back again in a week. While I was in the hospital it seemed that the authorities tried to starve us so we would want to go back to our regiments.

I got very hungry and one day while at Chickamauga I sauntered out to where some citizens were selling things that a hungry soldier likes and there I did one of the meanest tricks I was guilty of during the war. I never have felt just right about it to this good day. While I was standing around seeing others buying and eating I saw a woman selling half moon pies. She had an old horse and buggy and I walked up to her and said, "Madam, do you see that man walking off there?" pointing to a fellow about twenty steps away. She said she did and I said, "That fellow stole a lot of your pies." She went after him, and as soon as she started I commenced to pile half moon pies into my bosom. I stored away my goods and by the time she got through with the fellow I had business somewhere else, I went out behind a big pine tree and soon got outside the pies and went to my command.

Soon after this I was on the battle field the first day after my return. The Yankee soldiers that had been killed had not been buried and it was about a week as I recollect after the battle. The bodies were swollen so one could hardly see that they were men. They were actually as large as a horse. That was the worst sight I saw in the war. There was another thing I saw the same day, that I have always felt a delicacy in telling, that was our forces had gathered up all the small arms that was left on the field, a week before, the guns of our killed and wounded and the Yankees too, for we were in posession of the field, and the guns were racked up like cord wood. I never measured how long the ricks [stocks] were but feel safe in saying that they were seventy-five yards each.

In the battle of Chickamauga after I was wounded I went for the rear and in going back a cannon ball struck a limb on a big pine tree over me, I heard it hit the limb and stopped a second or so when the limb fell just in front of me. I believe I stepped over it the next step I took after it fell. I have always thought this was the closest call I had in the war.

Fighting in Georgia

We moved down to the railroad toward Atlanta and we had more or less fighting and skirmishing until we got to Atlanta. We had quite a hard fight at or near Resaca, Georgia. I will never forget the experience I had in fighting there. We were on one side of a hollow and the Yankees on top of the hill on the other side. The first evening we were there most of the fighting was an artillery duel and we hugged the ground closely as some of our batteries were up on the hill just behind us. [Confederate] Gen. [Leonidas] Polk and his escort came up on the hill behind the battery and we could hear the minie balls strike their horses and they soon left.

Two of my company, R.E. Garrett and James McGuire were lying down behind a log. A cannon ball went under the log and came out between them, covering them with dirt. The Yankees made it hot for us that evening as we did not have time to throw up works. That night we worked nearly all night and by morning we were fixed for them.

Just before 'day next morning I was detailed with others to go on picket duty about seventy-five yards down in front of our lines. I had been sick all night and was really in no condition to go, but this was no time to falter, so I went. Right down there on the picket line I had about the worst time I ever experienced. Our officer scattered us along about seventy-five yards apart. When day began to appear the Yankees began to shoot at us. I discovered a big pine stump near my post and I proceeded to get behind it. Then I was not safe as they could see me and commenced to cross fire on me. I saw that it was a bad proposition so I laid on my stomach and with my bayonet would dig up the sand and shove it out at each side and push the rest down with my feet and finally got a respectable war grave dug. I was still very sick, suffering from diarrhea and I was sleepy. The Yankees were still pegging away at me, a ball would strike the stump or a shell burst near me and wake me up but I would fall asleep as quickly as I would wake, so I laid there in the hot sun until about the middle of the afternoon when I saw if I stayed until night there would be a dead Rebel and he would have his grave already dug for him so I concluded to attempt to run back to the breastworks, about seventy-five rods up hill. You can imagine how sick I was to attempt such a dangerous trip for I was safe from Yankee bullets behind that stump. Well, I lit out as fast as I could run and every Yankee in sight took a shot at me. The bullets would zip by me and hit the ground but I kept pulling for the shore and when I got to breastworks I just simply fell over them down among the boys and not a scratch on me.

Soon after that the officer on picket duty was driven in and he had 18 bullet holes through his blanket but came out with a whole hide. A Lieutenant-Colonel was killed just on our right. Our regiment was not engaged but on our right they had it hot and heavy. After dark we commenced to retreat and marched until we got back as far as [Confederate] Gen. Joe Johnston wanted to go, formed again, and we kept it up until we landed south of the Chattahoochie river, with plenty of fighting all along.

I will tell some of the things I saw before we landed near Atlanta. While we were on Rocky Face Hill or Ridge, when we had nothing to do we would carry large rocks up on the ridge and turn them loose. The Yankee pickets were down on the side of the hill and the way those rocks would run and crash against trees was a caution. The Yankees could stand lead and cannon balls but the rocks were enough to break any of [Union General William] Sherman's lines that he could form.

It was fighting and falling back all the time. I will go south of the Chattahoochie river where the Rebel pickets were on the south side and the Yankees on the north. We got very friendly there and frequently some would cross over and do a lot of trading. The currency was coffee on the Yankee side and tobacco on the Rebel side. We would trade for U.S. stamps as we could send mail around by Richmond and Washington to our folks back in the territory occupied by the Federal army.

The way we did was to get a small flat rock, tie on a piece of tobacco and throw it across the river. The Yankees would wade out in the water and pick it up if it fell short. I was the only one on our side who could throw across the river and there was a red faced, red headed Yankee who was left handed who could throw over to our side. I remember on one occasion I put a piece of tobacco on a rock and threw it over saying "This is for the officer," and the soldier that got it took it to the officer. I saw him pull out a long book that he carried his papers in and handed the fellow five stamps. The red headed fellow threw them over to me.

One day while I was on picket there a handsome young fellow swam over. He was a fine fellow and I would be awful glad to meet him again. He came over on a trading expedition and while he was on our side I got in conversation with him. I told him I had a mother back in Tennessee who had not heard from me in a long time and asked him if he would mail a letter for me. He said he would and I wrote to my mother and he took it with him. On the way back he was so heavily loaded that he nearly drowned. We got him back and one of the boys went about a quarter of a mile and got a rail and he then made it all right. When the war was over and I got home I found the letter all right. He had mailed it as he said he would.

Chapter 4

The War from Home

Chapter Preface

The Civil War meant sacrifice for both Northern and Southern families, but in the South the fact that homes, farms, and a way of life were at stake brought about an intense commitment that Northern city dwellers could not match. As ordered by the Confederate government, all resources were devoted to the cause: fathers, husbands, and brothers for the fighting; food and livestock to feed the army; cotton to provide clothing; and money in the form of taxes and bonds to buy imported weapons and material. Southern women were expected to provide for their households, plant and harvest crops, and carry on as money and goods grew increasingly scarce. They also had to prepare for battle, as the vast majority of Civil War campaigns took place in Southern territory, with enemy soldiers terrorizing Confederate families and taking what food and household goods they could as the spoils of war.

The spirit of sacrifice did not reach the slave population, imagined by many Southerners as loyal and docile but nevertheless a source of dire fear and suspicion. Southern slaves were carefully watched, and any slaves found roaming away from their homes, or in the wrong place at the wrong time, were liable to be whipped or lynched as suspected spies and Union sympathizers. Nor did loyalty to the South prevent profiteers and speculators in the cities from taking advantage of rising prices and shortages. Private companies still moved and sold their goods for maximum profit, outside of government service; farmers still dodged government tax collectors; bandits ran riot over certain regions; and anti-secessionists resisted the Confederate cause by inaction and outright sabotage. Eventually shortages of food and necessities reached even the most productive Southern plantations, and the most ardent secessionists among Confederate women and men gave up hope.

Coward, Helpless Woman That I Am!

Sarah Morgan

> The daughter of a Louisiana judge, Sarah Morgan witnessed
> the occupation of New Orleans by Union forces under the
> command of Admiral David Farragut, who had captured the
> city in a daring raid in April, 1862. A perceptive observer,
> Ms. Morgan soon realized that the Confederacy was fighting
> a losing battle, and that the defiant people of New Orleans,
> especially the women of New Orleans, were holding to a past
> that was being slowly but surely destroyed by the guns and
> infantry of the Union army. In her bittersweet diary pages,
> she describes the sentiments of friends and family, the hopes
> and despair of people under siege, and memories of better,
> more peaceful days of the past.

*M*onday June 16th 1862.

There is no use in trying to break off journalizing
[diary writing], particularly in "these trying times." It has become a necessity to me. I believe I would go off in a rapid
decline if [Commander of the Occupation Forces in New Orleans General Benjamin] Butler took it in his head to prohibit
that, among other things. I get nervous and unhappy in thinking of the sad condition of the country and of the misery all
prophesy [h]as in store for us, get desperate to think I am fit
for nothing in the world, could not earn my daily bread, even,
and just before I reach the lowest ebb, I seize my pen, dash
off half a dozen lines, sing "Better days are coming" and

Excerpted from *The Civil War Diary of Sarah Morgan* (Athens: University of Georgia
Press, 1991).

Presto! [Brother-in-law] Richard [Drum] is himself again! O what a resource that and my books have been to me!

But to day I believe I am tired of life. I am weary of every thing. I wish I could find some "lodge in some vast wilderness" where I could be in peace and quiet; where I would never hear of war, or rumors of war, of lying, slandering, and all uncharitableness; where I could eat my bread in thanksgiving and trust God alone in all things; a place where I would never hear a woman talk politics or lay down the law—Bah! how it disgusts me! What paradise that would be, if such a place is to be found on earth! I am afraid it is not. What a consolation it is to remember there are no "Politics" in heaven! I reserve to myself the privilege of writing my opinions, since I trouble no one with the expression of them; the disgust I have experienced from listening to others, I hope will forever prevent me from becoming a "Patriotic woman." In my opinion, the Southern women, and some few of the men, have disgraced themselves by their rude, ill mannered behavior in many instances. I insist, that if the valor and chivalry of our men cannot save our country, I would rather have it conquered by a brave race, than owe its liberty to the Billingsgate [pretentious] oratory and demonstrations of some of these "ladies." If the women have the upper hand then, as they have now, I would not like to live in a country governed by such tongues.

Do I consider the female who could spit in a gentleman's face merely because he wore United States buttons, as a fit associate for me? Lieut. Biddle assured me he did not pass a street in New Orleans without being most grossly insulted by *ladies*. It was a friend of his into whose face a lady *spit* as he walked quietly by without looking at her. (Wonder if she did it to attract his attention?) He had the sense to apply to her husband and give him two minutes to apologize or die, and of course he chose the former. Such things are enough to disgust anyone. "Loud" women, what a contempt I have for you! How I despise your vulgarity!

Some of these Ultra Secessionists evidently very recently from "down East" who think themselves obliged to "kick up their heels over the Bonny blue flag" as Brother describes female patriotism, shriek out "What! see those vile Northerners pass patiently? No true Southerner could see it without rage! I could kill them! I hate them with all my soul, the murderers, liars, thieves, rascals! You are no Southerner if you do not hate them as much as I!" Ah ça! a true blue Yankee tell me that I, born and bred here, am no Southerner! I always think "It is well for you, my friend, to save your credit, else you might be suspected by some people, though your violence is enough for me." I always say "*You* may do as you please; my brothers are fighting for me, and doing their duty, so this excess of patriotism is unnecessary for me as my position is too well known to make any demonstrations requisite." I flatter myself that "tells."

Vanished Charity

This war has brought out wicked, malignant feelings that I did not believe could dwell in woman's heart. I see some with the holiest eyes, so holy one would think the very spirit of Charity lived in them and all Christian meekness, go off in a mad tirade of abuse and say with the holy eyes wonderously changed "I hope God will send down plague, Yellow fever, famine, on these vile Yankees, and that not one will escape death." O what unutterable horror that remark causes me as often as I hear it! I think of the many mothers, wives and sisters who wait as anxiously, pray as fervently in their far away lonesome homes for their dear ones, as we do here; I fancy them waiting day after day for the footsteps that will never come, growing more sad, lonely, and heartbroken as the days wear on; I think of how awful it would be to me if one would say "your brothers are dead," how it would crush all life and happiness out of me; and I say "God forgive these poor women! They know not what they say!" O woman! into what loathsome violence you have debased your holy mission! God will punish us for our hardheartedness.

Not a square off, in the new theater, lie more than a hundred sick soldiers. What woman has stretched out her hand to save them, to give them a cup of cold water? Where is the charity which should ignore nations and creeds, and administer help to the Indian or Heathen indifferently? Gone! all gone in Union versus Secession! *That* is what the American War has brought us. If I was independent, if I could work my own will without causing others to suffer for my deeds, I would not be poring over this stupid page, I would not be idly reading or sewing. I would put aside woman's trash, take up Woman's duty, and I would stand by some forsaken man and bid him God speed as he closes his dying eyes. *That* is Woman's mission! and not Preaching and Politics. I say I would, yet here I sit! O for liberty! the liberty that *dares* do what conscience dictates, and scorns all smaller rules!

If I could help these dying men! Yet it is as impossible as though I was a chained bear. I cant put out my hand. I am threatened with Coventry [ostracism] because I sent a custard to a sick man who is in the army, and with the anathema of society because I said if I could possibly do anything for Mr Biddle—at a distance—(he is sick) I would like to very much. . . . I would like to see the *man* who *dared* harm my father's daughter! But as he seems to think our conduct reflects on him, there is no alternative. Die, poor men, without a woman's hand to close your eyes! We women are too *patriotic* to help you! I look eagerly on, cry in my soul "I wish—"; you die, God judges me. Behold the woman who dares not risk private ties for God's glory and her professed religion! Coward, helpless woman that I am! If I was free!—

Remembering Will

June 17th 1862.

Yesterday, and day before, boats were constantly arriving, and troops embarking from here, destined for [the besieged city of] Vicksburg [Mississippi]. There will be another fight, and of course it will fall. I wish Will was out of it; I dont want him to die. I got the kindest, sweetest, letter from Will when Miriam came from Greenwell—! It was given to her by a guerilla on the road who asked if she was not Miss Sarah Morgan. I was glad to see that I was not forgotten; but there is no danger of his forgetting me. After his wife, I flatter myself there is no one on earth he loves more than Miriam and me. Mother does not believe in Platonic affection, she says, but here is a specimen of it. I would not have been any more willing to see Miriam marry him, than I would have been willing to—marry him myself! There now! Is that satisfactory enough? I had my own reasons for it; but I do believe that a more noble, generous heart than Will's, does not beat on earth. Indeed I like him! Perhaps it is because he was so connected with what was on the whole the happiest year of my happy life, 1860.

I remember well the first time I saw him. The week before Mattie was married Miriam went to Linwood for her health. She came back the Monday before the wedding, and told me of what a fine young man she had met twice there, a midshipman on a visit home. The next evening we were in the parlor with some young lady, when looking up, I saw a young man in citizen's dress just passing by Lydia's gate. "Here is Mr Pinkney" I said to Miriam. She would not mind, but went on talking. He passed the window, still not even looking at the house. I told her again it was he. Presently I heard a step on the balcony, and said "It *is* he; if you dont go out and meet him, I will!" She went out still incredulous, for she knew I had never seen him, and could not know him, and in another moment I was introduced to Mr Pinkney. How did I know him, I wonder? If he had been in uniform, I might have guessed; but he was in plain citizen's dress, as I said before. That was the last day of July; and from that day, to the first of September, there was hardly an hour of the day in which we did not see him, besides the occasional visits he and Howell used to pay us after, until one went to Annapolis, and the other to college.

That August at Linwood—! were we not happy? I wish we were all back again to 1860, that this war had never broken out, that Will was as merry and gay as he was then, and we were all back at Linwood dancing to the tunes from Lydia's, or Helen Carter's fingers, which would have made a puritan dance. I wish we could all be together for one day again! Ah me! I have not danced since the 29th of April

1861, I that danced forever, even while combing my hair! Howell and Will taught me to waltz then, and we danced at all times after, morning, noon, and night, just as we pleased. What rides we took! what walks! And moonlight nights walking around the circle and sitting on the balcony singing in the moonlight or dancing in the parlor! That was real pleasure; I only hope we will be as happy again.

Will played so beautifully on the violin, too. I never hear "[words lined through]" with out thinking of him; it is a sad air to me. Do you remember that warm breathless evening when after stifling us with the intense heat, the sun suddenly disappeared behind a great black cloud with a sudden rush the wind swept over the sugar cane bending the tops to the ground, and blew for an hour with the greatest violence? Do

The Legendary Exploits of Belle Boyd

The legendary career of Belle Boyd, Confederate spy, made her a postwar celebrity, a theatrical star and author of a best-selling autobiography. Boyd took advantage of prevailing social conventions, especially the notion that a woman could have little interest in military or political matters. She made abject prisoners of many a Yankee, and proved so useful to the Confederacy that Stonewall Jackson himself commissioned her as a captain and honorary aide-de-camp. In Mothers of Invention: Women of the Slave-holding South in the American Civil War, *Drew Gilpin Faust recounts some of Belle's exploits.*

B oyd first attracted public notice when in 1861, at age seventeen, she shot and killed a Yankee soldier for cursing her mother "in language as offensive as it is possible to conceive." Although his fellow enlisted men threatened to burn the Boyds' house, a group of officers investigating the matter concluded Belle had "done perfectly right." She was, they presumed, a lady exercising her right of defense against insult. For his failure to act the gentleman, the soldier had, you remember how, like a great baby, shaking with your terror of storms, wind especially, you sat in Helen Carter's lap speechless with fear while she rocked you in her arms in silent sympathy? and how Howell reasoned and coaxed, and Theodore [Will Pinkney's brother] stood silently by holding a glass of water and looking very miserable, and Wallace Badger cried aloud because you looked frightened, and Miriam laughed "'*Aint*' you ashamed?" While Will struck up "[words lined through]" and danced to his own music in illustration of the tune while exhorting, begging, insisting that you would laugh just once, there was no danger?. . .

June 18th.

How long, O how long is it since I have laid down in peace, thinking "this night I will rest in safety?" Certainly

---

it seemed, deserved to die.

Less than a week after this incident the Yankees discovered Boyd gathering information in the course of flirtatious conversations with Federal soldiers and passing it on to Confederate officials. Once again Boyd was spared, as the commanding colonel chose only to read her the article of war indicating such actions to be punishable by death. Boyd's successful espionage career was launched.

As she described her exploits over the next three years, nearly every triumph derived from her use of Yankee assumptions about womanhood to entrap her unsuspecting foes. When her horse ran away into Federal lines near Martinsburg, she abjectly requested permission to return home from her Union captors. Gallant Yankee cavalrymen offered to escort the lady back across the lines, and she gratefully accepted. But when they reached the Confederate pickets, Boyd delivered the Union soldiers as prisoners. Having extracted the courtesy of safe passage from the Yankees, she declined to offer them the same. "I consoled myself that, 'all was fair in love and war,'" she explained.

Drew Gilpin Faust, *Mothers of Invention: Women of the Slaveholding South in the American Civil War.* Chapel Hill: University of North Carolina Press, 1996.

not since the fall of Fort Jackson [Mississippi, on May 14, 1863]. If left to myself, I would not anticipate evil, but would quietly await the issue of all these dreadful events; but when I hear men who certainly should know better than I, express their belief that in twenty four hours the town will be laid in ashes, I begin to grow uneasy, and think it must be so, since they say it. These last few days, since the news arrived of the intervention of the English and French, I have alternately risen and fallen from the depth of despair to the height of delight and expectation, as the probability of another Exodus diminishes and peace appears more probable. If these men would not prophesy the burning of the city, I would be perfectly satisfied; what is the use of making women and children unnecessarily unhappy? I am very much afraid it will produce a very unpleasant effect on me, making me believe after a while only a small proportion of what they say, and think that perhaps I myself know as much as they, after all—which will look dreadfully conceited.

Annoyed by these constantly expressed beliefs, this morning I put several changes of clothes in a large bag to await the final issue; so if I must run, I will have a change of clean linen *this* time, for the next time it is shelled B.R. [Baton Rouge, Louisiana] will certainly disappear from the face of creation. My better sense tells me there is very little probability of such an event; the sensation mongers cry it is inevitable; can I be wiser than the rest? Of course they must know. All loyal patriots, who own no property here, cry loudly "Burn the town down! I'll help!" Thanks, Messieurs.

The Battle Raged All Day

Cornelia Peake McDonald

A resident of Winchester, Virginia, at the northern end of the Shenandoah Valley, Cornelia Peake McDonald lived in one of the Confederacy's most fought-over regions, a place occupied, attacked, defended, and abandoned by Union and Confederate forces throughout most of the war. Of her book, *A Woman's Civil War*, editor Minrose C. Gwin says McDonald "records a distinctly female battle of her own: the struggle for survival and the care of nine children . . . a gripping record of a white Southern woman's struggle in the midst of chaos to provide nurturance and shelter—a safe place—for herself and her family."

In March 1862, the Civil War came directly to McDonald's doorstep as the opposing armies fought for position in and around Winchester.

12 th—The battle raged all day in sight of town, shells screaming through the air so constantly that for some time we dared not go out. I sent the servant girl, Nannie, to town on an errand and as she came near the gate a shell burst in front of her. She was terribly frightened, and quickened her steps; when she reached the house, panting, she remarked that it was the last time she was going to town; and I do not wonder, for it was no holiday spectacle. The hardest fighting was on the old battlefield of Kernstown where [Stonewall] Jackson fought them a little more than a year

Excerpted from the diary entries of Cornelia Peake McDonald, as they appear in *A Woman's Civil War: A Diary, with Reminiscences of the War, from March 1862*, edited by Minrose C. Gwin (Madison: University of Wisconsin Press, 1992).

ago, and by his strategy changed their entire plans.

The Yankee soldiers say that [Union Brigadier General R.H.] Milroy will certainly destroy the town if he is hard pressed. A man told me that Lee has driven [Union General Joseph] Hooker into Alexandria and from another source I hear that [Confederate Brigadier General Isaac R.] Trimble is in Front Royal and that Berryville is in our possession. We have a large force near here and tomorrow there will be a severe fight. There will be a struggle for possession of the town and fort. The town may be destroyed as they threaten, but we can only hope and pray for the best. I shall sleep tonight, that is I shall try, to be ready for what tomorrow may bring. I can scarcely hope to see our men so soon.

Watching the Battle

14th—Victory! thanks to our Father in Heaven; our enemies are at last powerless to harm us. Musketry and cannon firing began early in the morning, but not very near us. Mrs. Dailey came over to stay with me as her house was so unprotected, and was within range of the shells. We sat together in the dining room before the windows looking to the West; and it seemed so strange to sit quietly in a rocking chair and watch the progress of a battle. We were yet on the outskirts, and could see the troops deploying, skirmish lines thrown forward and mounted men galloping from one point to another, batteries wheeling into position, and every now and then the thunder of cannon and the shriek of shell. Still they were at a distance, and there we sat, all that sweet June morning, and watched and listened, and occasionally shrank a little when a shell from a battery on the same hill opposite to the house, that one year ago our troops stormed and took, and sent its defenders panic-stricken down the hillside or rolled them in the dust; when a shell came crashing through the trees near the house, and reminded us that we were in danger. Thick and fast they presently came, one after another. A Confederate battery has possession of the hill, and the answering shots are from the fort. We are just in their path. Our battery is south of us, and the fort slightly east of north. So they go, whizzing screaming, and coming down with a dreadful thud or crash and then burst. We hold our breath and cover our eyes till they pass. I gather all the children in till the firing ceases.

About noon there is comparative quiet, and Mrs. Dailey goes home with her children. I begin to feel that the effort has failed and the Confederates are retiring; but it is only the lull before another greater storm. About three o'clock I went out into the front porch to see what was going on. The children were playing in the yard. High on the hill opposite the same battery spouted flame and smoke, and the fort slowly responded. Men were passing and repassing, and many looking pale and anxious. Some wearily dropped down and went to sleep under the trees. The two little boys, Donald and Roy, seemed to forget the shells and were playing in the yard, running and catching the men as they passed, saying, "I take you prisoner." Though there was a cessation of the firing in a great measure, the faces of the passing groups of men, or stragglers, as they were, did not look less anxious. I heard one officer telling another that [Union General James A.] Mulligan was coming from Cumberland to relieve them. Then I felt comfortable to know that they needed relief.

Pale Flying Men

I was, up to that time ignorant of the state of affairs, and of all except what was to be seen from my own point of observation. At five o'clock I again went and stood on the porch, dejectedly fancying that the attempt had failed, and we were again left to our fate. Two officers stood within hearing leaning against a tree, a linden tree that grew close to the house door, and filled the air with its perfume. They were pale and looked disturbed as they talked to each other in a low tone. Suddenly a blaze of fire from those western hills from which Mulligan was to issue for their relief. "That is Mulligan," said one; "Mulligan has come," echoed all around. But the shout was suddenly silenced when they saw the direction in which the balls were sent. Straight into their works they plunged, and soon a dusky line was seen making its way toward their outer works. Crashing of cannon and rattling of musketry till those were taken, and then the guns were turned on the fort. Then it seemed as if shells and cannon balls poured from every direction at once. One battery from the hill opposite our house rushed down and through our yard, their horses wounded and bleeding, and men wounded also, and pale with fright. More artillery and more horses and pale flying men rush by where I stood. Hurrying groups of stragglers, and officers without swords, and some bareheaded. They were all hastening up to the fort which they had imagined was a place of safety. Gen. Milroy with a few of his body guard galloped by; I saw his pale agitated face as he passed within ten feet of me, and felt sorry for him; so following my impulse of being kind I bowed to him; from pure sympathy; for I really did at the time feel for his misfortunes, though I would not have averted them. He may have thought it a piece of mock respect, but whatever he thought or felt, he bowed low, till his plume almost touched his horse's mane. The fort all the time was sending its huge shot and shell over and through the town to where our troops were, and from the west proceeded a blaze of fire and a cloud of smoke that carried death into their stronghold into which they were crowding by hundreds.

Comforting the Wounded

Until now they seemed to be flying to the fort for safety, and it was pitiable to see them as they were hurrying by, turn their eyes to the west, pause and look bewildered, then look around for a place of safety, and finally avail themselves of the only spot the shells did not reach, the angle of our house. I had retreated there with my children when the shots and shells began to fly so fast, and burst all around the house; and then as I sat on the porch bench men came crowding in. Now a surgeon bringing a wounded man; he, the surgeon, looks so humbled and frightened that I did not at first recognize in him the same one who had behaved so insultingly last winter when he demanded my house. He goes away, but soon comes back more frightened and agitated than ever.

They talk openly of being surrounded. The soldiers say they will stay and be captured.

I tried to comfort the wounded man who sat on the bench by me, but he was past comfort; a ball was lodged in his throat and he sat with his poor wretched face distorted with pain through all those weary hours; close to me he was and the hard breathing as he struggled to keep the blood from choking him was dreadful to hear. Crowd after crowd of men continued to pour into the porch till it was packed full; then they crowded as close as they could get, to be sheltered by the angle of the house. Ambulances were backed up to let out their loads of wounded, and horses reared frantic with pain from their bleeding wounds. Some were streaming with blood, and looking wild, with their poor eyes stretched wide with pain and fright. All made an effort to crowd in there and the close atmosphere was almost suffocating. I could not move, or hide the dreadful sights from my eyes. . . .

Capture

15th—I did not lock my chamber door and then went to bed and slept as soundly as I ever did in my life. The scenes of the day floated through my brain all night, the maneuvering troops scudding over the hills, shells flying, men rushing back and forth, artillery, infantry and ambulances confusedly hurrying by, and amidst it all my little ones playing in the yard in the bright summer sunshine, as happy and unconcerned as if all was peace around them. Poor little things, they have long been used to scenes of strife and confusion, and I suppose it now seems to them the natural course of things.

I was wakened at dawn by cannon, dressed and went down; the floor was still covered with sleeping men. Their sleep was deep for they were very weary I suppose. At any rate I had to push one with my foot to arouse him and told him to awake the others. I waited for them to go, and invited them to depart, but still they lingered. The cannon had ceased. I went to the front door and there filing into the yard was a column of grey coats! I could not help it, but waved my handkerchief high over my head. They came up and halted before the door. I told an officer the Yankees were in the house; he asked me to send them out. I told them to go, and each one laid his musket down and marched sadly out.

They marched them off, and I ran through the wet grass up to the top of the hill where the fort was. I went to it. The United States flag was waving in the morning breeze, but not a soldier was to be seen. They had all gone and destroyed nothing. I stood looking with amazement at the immense work they had constructed so near me and I had never seen it before; never dared to go in that direction. Some one came galloping up the hill. It was Capt. Richardson. He told me of [Confederate General Jubal] Early's flank movement; he was with him. The Louisiana brigade charged the first outwork and took it, then turned the guns on the fort. That was the time when the firing was heaviest, and the terror so great. General Gordon and his staff soon come riding up, and I turn and go down the hill.

Went in town this afternoon; the girls told me that in the early morning, long before light, many ladies expecting our men to come in had assembled in the streets to greet them; and as the marching column drew near they with one accord burst into singing "The Bonnie Blue Flag." The bands all stopped, and the troops stood still till they had finished, and then their shouts rent the air, caps were waved, and hurrahs resounded. Some Yankee prisoners were standing on the Hotel porch, and one was heard to say the men could fight when they knew such a welcome awaited them.

Lieut. Richardson came to tea; he gave me a description of their approach to the town. Milroy evacuated the fort during the night and stole away leaving the flag flying. All his force was captured about seven miles from town. We captured all their baggage, even their officers' trunks and mess chests. Milroy escaped alone by a byroad. Our men threaten to hang him if they can catch him on account of his treatment of the people of the town. Today I saw forty-five hundred prisoners marched by. Many faces I recognized as those I have had to look at all the winter.

15th—This afternoon a squad of Confederates marched up to the door with a woe begone looking surgeon in the midst of them. When they got him to the door they sent for me to ask if he was the one who behaved so badly to me last winter. I recognized in him the one who had been kind and serviceable in helping me to take care of Aunt Winnie when she was ill, and was glad to testify in his favour. He had asked them to bring him to me that I might convince them that he had not been offensive in his behavior. Every surgeon they had taken was ironed and sent to Richmond to the Libby prison. Dr. Patton was my man, and I think they got him, but for fear of missing him they took all.

16th—Went to town to help make a Confederate flag out of two captured ones. Made it by the new pattern. White flag with the battle flag for the Union. We had to work hard for Gen. Ewell waited to see it float before he left for Pennsylvania. I stood on Mrs. Hopkins' porch holding it up to see how it looked, when Mr. Williams passed. Men were going by, Yankees and all. "It is imprudent," said Mr. Williams, "to let them see you with it." I laughed at his fears, feeling so triumphant, and so secure that our army was there for good.

We, Too, Loved the Union

Parthenia Antoinette Hague

A young schoolteacher, Parthenia Antoinette Hague lived in
southern Alabama, in the heart of the plantation society and
one of the regions most loyal to secession and to the Confederacy. Hague, whose three brothers fought for the South,
describes her feelings of regret and worry over leaving the
Union. The blockade of southern ports by a Union fleet
means that the Alabamians must depend on their own
resourcefulness to survive, an effort to preserve what Hague
sees as a paradise on earth. She also reveals a strong pride in
the South's gentility and hospitality, extended even to treach-
erous northern preachers come to spy on the homes of her
neighbors.

O n a glorious sunshiny morning in the early summer of
1861 I was on my way to the school-house on the plantation of a gentleman who lived near Eufaula, Alabama, and
in whose service I remained during the period of the war.

As I was nearing the little school-room on a rising knoll,
all shaded with great oaks and sentineled with tall pines, I
heard skipping feet behind me, and one of my scholars exclaiming, "Here is a letter for you, Miss A——! It has just
been brought from the office by 'Ed'"—the negro boy who
was sent every morning for the mail.

A glance at the handwriting gave me to know it was from
my father. I soon came to a pause in the school path: for my

Excerpted from *A Blockaded Family: Life in Southern Alabama During the Civil War*, by
Parthenia Antoinette Hague (Boston: Houghton Mifflin, 1888).

father wrote that my brothers were preparing to start for Richmond, Virginia, as soldiers of our new formed Southern Confederacy. As he wished to have all his children united under his roof, before the boys went away, my father earnestly desired me to ask leave of absence for a few days, so that I might join the home circle also.

The suspending of the school was easily arranged, and I was soon at home assisting in preparing my brothers for military service, little dreaming they were about to enter into a four-years' conflict!

But oh, how clearly even now I read every milestone of that convulsed period, as I look back upon it after a quarter of a century! Our soldiers, in their new gray uniforms, all aglow with fiery patriotism, fearing ere they should join battle that the last booming cannon would have ceased to reverberate among the mountains, hills, and valleys of "Old Virginia." The blue cockades streaming in the wind, while Southern songs, inspirations of the moment, were heard on all sides: "We conquer or die," and "Farewell to Brother Jonathan," leading with fervent ardor.

Southern Sentiments

While the war was in progress, it so happened that I was far removed from the seaboard and border States, in southern Alabama, where our people, encompassed and blockaded by the Federal forces, were most sadly straitened and distressed. It is of the exigencies [necessities] of that stormy day, as hydra-headed they rose to view, that I have to write; of the many expedients to which we were reduced on our ever-narrowing territory, daily growing not only smaller, but less and less adequate for the sustenance of ourselves, our soldiers, and the Northern prisoners who were cast upon us by the fortunes of war.

Blame us not too severely, you who fought on the Union side; we, too, loved the Union our great and good Washington bequeathed us: with what deep devotion God knoweth. But, as Satan sagely remarks in the Book of Job, "all that a man hath will he give for his life.". . .

A Spy for John Brown

I well remember the day when word came with lightning speed over the wires, "The State of Georgia"—my native State, one of the original thirteen of revolutionary fame—"is out of the Union." I also remember that we were by no means elated at the thought that our own noble commonwealth had seceded from the sisterhood of states. Feelings of sadness, rather, somewhat akin to those of the Peri outside the gate of Paradise, overcame us, but we thought and said, Come weal or woe, success or adversity, we will willingly go down or rise with the cause we have embraced. And at that moment an unpleasant recollection rushed to mind, which caused me to think that perhaps, after all, secession was not so very bad. I remembered a temperance lecturer from one of the New England States, who came to our settlement and who was kindly received and warmly welcomed in our Southern homes. There was nothing too good for this temperance lecturer from the far North. He was given earnest and attentive audiences, with never a thought that in the guise of the temperance reformer his one sole purpose was to make a secret survey of our county, to ascertain which settlements were most densely populated with slaves, for the already maturing uprising of the blacks against the whites.

After the failure of the insurrection at Harper's Ferry [staged by violent abolitionist John Brown], we saw with sorrow deep-felt that the three places in our own county which were known all too well to be most thickly peopled with slaves were marked on John Brown's map of blood and massacre, as the first spots for the negro uprising for the extermination of the Southern whites.

A Funereal Voyage

When my brothers had left for Virginia, I started again for southern Alabama, to renew my school duties. As the train sped onward through the tall, long-leaved pines and funereal cypress-trees rising here and there on either side, a feeling of homesick desolation gathered as a thick mist around me, with vague and undefined forebodings of sorrows in store for us. . . .

As the train gathered itself up in the village of Hurtville, the inky black clouds, flashes of almost blinding lightning, and heavy peals of rolling thunder told that the tempest was unchained.

I still had a distance of fourteen or fifteen miles to travel by the hack [horse-drawn carriage] before I should reach my school. But as the storm began to increase so much in violence, I deemed it advisable to remain in Hurtville for the night. On inquiring for a place to stop at for the night I was directed to Mrs. Hurt, whose spacious mansion and large and beautiful flower yard and grounds stood fair to view from the little village depot.

A Celebration

Hitherto I had passed the village by, in my trips home and back to school again during my vacation days, so that I was altogether a stranger in the home of Mrs. Hurt, but on making her acquaintance was pleased to find her most kind and generous. My quiet satisfaction was further augmented by a loved school companion stepping into the room most unexpectedly, ere I had been seated half an hour. It was a glad surprise for both. Her father and mother lived in the village, and as the violent wind and rain storm had made roads and bridges impassable for the time being, I accepted the invitation of my friend to spend the time of my detention with her.

One pleasing episode of that visit yet clings to memory. It so happened that one of the negro girls of the house was to be married the very week I was detained. Preparations in various ways had been making for several days before the celebration of the ceremony. Dear Winnie, if still a sojourner here, and you chance to see these lines, I know your memory with mine will turn back on the wheels of time to that afternoon, when we were seated on the colonnade of your father's house. With flowers scattered all around, our laps and hands full, we twined the wreath for the negro girl, the bride elect for the evening. When twilight had deepened into darkness, the bride was called into your room to make ready for the marriage. When fully robed in her wedding garment, she was inspected by each and every member of the household, and judged to be quite *au fait*. But Winnie pulled off her own watch and chain, together with her bracelets, and with these further adorned the bride. She was married in the wide hall of her master's house, for having been raised in the house almost from her cradle, her marriage taking place in one of the cabins was not to be thought of.

Directly under the supervision of the mistress of the house, a supper that would have been pleasing to the taste of an epicure [gourmet] was served on tables placed out in the smooth gravelly yard. Then after the feasting was over, a round of merry plays, interspersed with the merrier songs and dance, followed. Perhaps no happier beings existed that night. It was like a vision of fairy-land. The full moon chosen for the occasion rode in silent majesty across the star-gemmed heavens; fleecy white clouds flitted like shadowy phantoms across its silvery path; the dark pines, half in shadow, half in sheen, loomed vast and giant-like on the outskirts of the village. In the deeper forest could be heard the weird notes of the whip-poor-wills. The pleasing strains of the violin, the thrumming of the banjo, accompanied by many negro voices, awoke the sleeping echoes. From the front colonnade, before us lay the slumbering village all so quietly under the starry firmament. We listened there to the mellow peals of negro laughter, to their strange songs, mingling with the strains of the violin, and the low breathing of the night wind in the forest.

The Substitute Preacher

As we roam back in the past, events of earlier days rise in bright view to mind; one link in memory's chain runs into another. I cannot forbear here referring to an incident which occurred a few years before the civil war. There came to our settlement from the North, three cultured, refined, and educated ladies as schoolteachers. Their first Sabbath of worship in the South was at the Mount Olive Baptist church, in

Harris County, Georgia. The pastor of the church, for some unknown cause, failed to appear at the hour appointed for service. We waited for some time and still no preacher. Then the good old deacon, known by all as "Uncle Billy" Moore, who had lived by reason of strength beyond the allotted threescore and ten, arose, and said, as the hour for service was passing, as the minister's arrival seemed doubtful, and as the congregation had all assembled, he would suggest that Uncle Sol Mitchell, an old and honored negro, preach for us, as he was present, and a member and preacher in good standing in the Mount Olive church. There was not even a shadow of an objection to the negro slave's occupying the pulpit, as our friends from the far North were witness. Ah, friends of the Green Mountain [Vermont], and Bay State [Massachusetts], you will, if yet in the flesh, remember with me that Sabbath so long ago in the South, when the negro slave walked up to the pulpit, opened the hymn-book, and announced the old sacred song:

> "When I can read my title clear,
> To mansions in the skies."

I remember how loudly my dear father tried to sing—though only a poor singer—just because Uncle Sol was going to preach; how Sol gave the verses out by couplets to be sung, as was the custom then in the country. All joined in singing that sacred song, and bowed the knee when Uncle Sol said, "Let us pray." I am very sure I have never knelt with more humble devotion and reverence than on that Sabbath morning.

Roads and bridges having been made passable after the storm, I said the "Good-by" to the friends I had found in the pleasant country village, and resumed my journey. . . .

Work Enough to Be Done

In the near distance the home of my generous employer rose to view, in every respect the characteristic Southern home, with its wide halls, long and broad colonnade, large and airy rooms, the yard a park in itself, fruits and flowers abounding. Here there was little or nothing to remind us of the impending conflict. We were far from the border States and remote from the seaboard. We had surmised that our sequestered vale [valley] must have been the spot where the Indian chief and his braves thrust their tomahawks deep down in the soil, with their "Alabama, here we rest!" But soon it came home to us, as the earnestness of the strife began to be realized, and when we found ourselves encompassed by the Federal blockade, that we had to depend altogether upon our own resources; and no sooner had the stern facts of the situation forced themselves upon us, than we joined with zealous determination to make the best of our position, and to aid the cause our convictions impressed on us as right and just. And if up to that time, in the South, many had engaged in work purely as a matter of choice, there were none, even the wealthiest, who had not been taught that labor was honorable, and who had very clear ideas of how work must be done; so when our misfortunes came, we were by no means found wanting in any of the qualities that were necessary for our changed circumstances.

Surely there was work enough to be done. Our soldiers had to be fed and clothed; our home ones had to be fed and clothed. All clothing and provisions for the slaves had to be produced and manufactured at home. Leather had to be of our own tanning; all munitions of war were to be manufactured inside the blockade. The huge bales of kerseys [coarse wool], osnaburgs [cotton for sacks and simple clothing], and boxes of heavy brogan-shoes [ankle-high work shoes], which had been shipped from the North to clothe and shoe the slaves, were things of the past. Up to the beginning of the war we had been dependent on the North for almost everything eaten and worn. Cotton was cultivated in the South almost universally before the war, it was marketed in the North, it was manufactured there, and then returned in various kinds of cloth-material to us.

Wartime Slavery in Missouri

Henry Clay Bruce

Feeling no loyalty to the South that had made captives of them, the slaves of the Confederacy lived in fear of retribution by their masters and in hope of a Union victory that would destroy the region where they lived. In the border state of Missouri, the grim struggle between Union and Confederate sympathizers took a brutal toll on the slaves, who were watched, suspected, and often hunted down by poor whites seeking bounty payments and other favors in the struggle to survive and support their own families. And as Confederate recruits left the territory they were replaced by bandits whose only goal was the pillage of unguarded farms and unwary travellers.

In his memoir *The New Man,* Henry Clay Bruce relates the tragic events suffered by his fellow slaves, the sympathetic actions of his owner, as well as his risky romance with a young slave woman and an escape to the frontier territory of Kansas.

D uring the years of 1860 and 1861, the slaves had to keep very mum and always on their masters' land, because patrols were put out in every township with authority to punish slaves with the lash, if found off their masters' premises after dark without a written pass from them. Patrol duty was always performed by the poor whites, who took great pride in the whipping of a slave. . . . They whipped

Excerpted from "The New Man: Twenty-nine Years a Slave. Twenty-nine Years a Free Man," by Henry Clay Bruce, from *Documenting the American South; or, The Southern Experience in Nineteenth-Century America*, available at http://metalab.unc.edu/docsouth/ bruce/bruce.html.

some slaves so unmercifully that their masters' attention was called to it, so that they met and issued an order to patrols, that in punishing a slave captured no skin should be broken nor blood brought out by the lash. There being no positive law of patrolling, it having existed as a custom to please a few mean slave holders, many men whose names I can give, would not submit to it, and threatened to punish any man or set of men interfering in any way with their slaves, although found off their lands. Of course the patrols carefully avoided such men's slaves wherever seen.

I have heard of many jokes played on these patrols by slaves, tending to show how easy it was to fool them, because they were as a rule illiterate, and of course could not read writing. The slaves knowing this would take a portion of a letter picked up and palm it off on them as a pass when arrested. The captain would take it, look it over wisely, then hand it telling the slave to go. Others would secure a pass from their master, get some one who could read writing to erase the day and month, then use it indefinitely, while others would get their young master or mistress to write them a pass whenever they wanted to go out, signing their father's name.

In order that the reader may clearly understand why slaves had to resort to so many tricks to get a pass, I will state that masters objected to giving passes often, upon the ground that they wanted the slave to stay at home and take his rest which he could not get if out often after dark. . . .

I remember [a] ball given at Day's Mill, near Brunswick, early in 1861, which I attended, and left about eleven o'clock that night. Later, a man named Price, without law or authority, as he lived in the city and was not an officer thereof, gathered a squad of roughs and went to the Mill and surrounded the ballroom. They ordered all who had passes to come forward, and they were allowed to go free. There were five men and one girl without a pass left in the room. The white men stood in the doorway, intending to whip each Negro and pass him out. They had given the order for each one to take off his shirt. There was a fellow whose name, for prudential reasons, I will call John Smith, who got a shovel and threw fire coals, one shovelful after another, at the patrols. The lights had been extinguished; some of them got burnt in the face and neck badly, while others got clothing burnt. This cleared the way, and the Negroes, even the women, escaped. They never found the man who threw the fire. I remember that they offered a reward to other slaves to betray the one who threw it. . . .

Exciting Times

Slaves were much truer to one another in those days than they have been since made free, and I am unable to assign any reason for it, yet it is a fact, nevertheless, and as further proof of it, I will state, that they would listen carefully to what they heard their owners say while talking to each other on political matters, or about the fault of another slave, and as soon as opportunity would admit, go to the quarters and warn the slave of his danger, and tell what they had heard the master say about the politics of the country.

The Colored people could meet and talk over what they had heard about the latest battle and what Mr. Lincoln had said, and the chances of their freedom, for they understood the war to be for their freedom solely, and prayed earnestly and often for the success of the Union cause. When the news came that a battle was fought and won by Union troops, they rejoiced, and were correspondingly depressed when they saw their masters rejoicing, for they knew the cause thereof. As I have stated before, slaves who could read and could buy newspapers, thereby obtained the latest news and kept their friends posted, and from mouth to ear the news was carried from farm to farm, without the knowledge of masters. There were no Judases among them during those exciting times.

After the war had commenced, about the spring of 1862, and troops of both sides were often passing through that county, it was not safe for patrols to be out hunting Negroes, and the system came to an end, never to be revived. The regular confederate troops raised in that and adjoining counties went South as fast as recruited, so that only bushwhackers [bandits] remained, and they were a source of annoyance to

Union men and Union troops of that county up to the fall and winter of 1864, when they were effectually cleaned out. Many of these men claimed to be loyal [i.e., Unionist], especially so in public and at their homes in the day time, in order to be protected, while at heart they were disloyal, aiding bushwhackers not only with ammunition, rations, and information as to when and where Union troops would pass, but with their presence at night on the roadside, shooting at Union citizens and soldiers while passing. They would select some safe spot where a returned fire would not reach them.

The spirit of secession was almost as strong in that county in 1861, as it was in South Carolina, and when Fort Sumter was fired upon, Col. Pugh Price, of Brunswick, hung out the confederate flag, and called for volunteers. There were two companies raised who went South, one of which was commanded by Capt. J.W. Price. That county furnished its full share to the confederate army, composed largely of the best blood, men who were willing to shoot and be shot at in the open field of battle.

The Lincoln Man

There was a man named James Long, a plasterer by trade, who was a noisy fellow, and who cast the only vote Lincoln received in that county. When called upon to give his reasons for so doing, he stated that he did it for fun; he then and there cursed Lincoln in language quite strong, and said that he ought to be assassinated. A year later, a loyal man had to be appointed postmaster at Brunswick, and then this man Long came forward as the only original Lincoln man, stating that his vote represented his sentiments, and that his former denial was caused by intimidation. He got the appointment, and in a year or two was arrested, tried, convicted and sentenced to the penitentiary for misappropriation of government money. But the secessionists lost a friend in him, because it was believed by Union men that he was not of them, and it was charged that he aided the rebels in every way possible, even to rifling Union men's letters, and giving their contents to rebels.

But this man's downfall was a blessing to some extent, to the Colored people who received mail through that office, for he would not give them their mail, but held it and delivered it to their masters. Our family had no trouble in this respect, for our master would bring our letters unopened and deliver them without question. I remember getting one from my brother, B.K. Bruce, who was in Lawrence, Kan., at the time of the [Confederate Raider William Clarke Quantrill] raid, in 1863, which he brought from town, and waited to hear how B.K. Bruce escaped being killed in the Lawrence massacre.

Negro Traders

From 1862 to the close of the war, slave property in the state of Missouri was almost a dead weight to the owner; he could not sell because there were no buyers. The business of the Negro trader was at an end, due to the want of a market. He could not get through the Union lines South with his property, that being his market. There was a man named White, usually called "Negro-trader White," who travelled over the state, buying Negroes like mules for the southern market, and when he had secured a hundred or more, he would take them, handcuffed together, to the South. He or his agents attended all sales where Negroes were to be sold without conditions. The sentiment against selling Negroes to traders was quite strong and there were many who would not sell at all, unless forced by circumstances over which they had no control, and would cry with the Negroes at parting. A Negro sold to a trader would bring from one to three hundred dollars more money.

I recall a case where a master was on a note [loan] as surety, and had the same, which was a large sum, to pay at maturity, and to do so he was forced to sell a young girl to raise the cash. He sent for Negro-trader White, and the sale was made in the city without his wife's knowledge, but when he attempted to deliver her, his wife and children clung to the girl and would not let her go. When White saw he could not get his Negro, he demanded a return of his money, which the seller had applied on the note and could not get back. The matter was finally settled in some way; at any rate the girl was not sold, and was in that county until 1864.

The Negro trader usually bought all Negroes who had committed murder or other crimes, for which public whipping was not considered sufficient punishment. Slaves usually got scared when it became known that Negro-trader White was in the community. The owners used White's name as a threat to scare the Negroes when they had violated some rule. "I'll sell you to the Negro trader, if you don't do better" was often as good or better punishment than the lash, for the slave dreaded being sold South, worse than the Russians do banishment to Siberia.

Excitement, such as I had never seen, existed not alone with the white people, but with the slaves as well. Work, such as had usually been performed, almost ceased; slaves worked as they pleased, and their masters were powerless to force them, due largely to the fact that the white people were divided in sentiment. Those who remained loyal advised the slaves who belonged to those called disloyal, not to work for men who had gone or sent their sons South, to fight against the government. Slaves believed, deep down in their souls, that the government was fighting for their freedom, and it was useless for masters to tell them differently. They would leave home in search of work, and usually found it, with small pay, with some Union man and often without pay for weeks at a time, but his master had to clothe him as he had always done, and in some cases pay his own slave for his work.

Confiscations

Near the close of 1863, the Union men were on top, and the disloyal or southern sympathizer had to submit to everything. The lower class of so-called Union men almost openly robbed rebel sympathizers by going to their farms, dressed and armed as soldiers, taking such stock as they wanted, which the owner was powerless to prevent; in fact he would have been killed had he attempted it. The period had been reached when the master found his slave to be his best and truest friend, because it often happened that he was forced for self-protection to hide his valuables from these prowlers, and knowing that their quarters would not be invaded, he placed his precious property in their hands for safe keeping.

I remained on our farm, managing it as I had done in past years, but I saw that the time had about come when I could do so no longer. I saw men, whose names I could state, take from our farm hogs, cattle, and horses without permission and without paying for them, under the pretense that it was a military necessity. Of course no such necessity existed, and the government received no benefit therefrom.

I remember that W.B. Bruce [Henry's master] owned a fine lot of horses and cattle in 1862, but by March, 1864, they had all or nearly all been taken, without his consent, and often without his knowledge. I speak of only two cases of this kind, because I have personal knowledge of them. After the war, many of these men who had lost their property, other than slaves, presented claims against the government for property supposed to have been confiscated or appropriated to the use of Uncle Sam, and these claimants were honest in their belief that their property was so taken, when, as a matter of fact, it was taken by thieves, dressed in uniform for the purpose of deception, men who were not in the Union army, and the stolen property was used for their own personal benefit. W.B. Bruce is now living and can, if he will, testify to the truthfulness of what I state here. . . .

Escape and Elopement

The enlistment of Colored men for the army commenced in Chariton County, Missouri, early in December, 1863, and any slave man who desired to be a soldier and fight for freedom, had an opportunity to do so. Certain men said to be recruiting officers from Iowa, came to Brunswick, to enlist Colored men for the United States Army, who were to be accredited not to Missouri, but to certain townships in Iowa, in order to avoid a draft there. I am unable to state the number of Colored men who enlisted in that county during the period from December, 1863, until the close of enlistments in the spring of 1865, but I am sure it was large. I had some trouble with these enlisted men, which was as follows: Being in the United States service themselves, they thought it no more than right to press in every young man they could find, being secretly aided by these white officers, who, I learned afterwards, received a certain sum of money for each recruit raised and accredited as above described. These Colored men scoured the county in search of young men for soldiers, causing me to sleep out of nights and hide from them in the daytime. I was afraid to go to town while they were there, and greatly relieved when a company was filled out and left for some point in Iowa.

Our owner did not want us to leave him and used every persuasive means possible to prevent it. He gave every grown person a free pass, and agreed to give me fifteen dollars per month, with board and clothing, if I would remain with him on the farm, an offer which I had accepted to take effect January 1, 1864. But by March of that year I saw that it could not be carried out, and concluded to go to Kansas. I might have remained and induced others to do so and made the crop, which would have been of little benefit to him, as it would have been spirited away. I made the agreement in good faith, but when I saw that it could not be fulfilled had not the courage to tell him that I was going to leave him.

I was engaged to marry a girl belonging to a man named Allen Farmer, who was opposed to it on the ground, as I was afterwards informed, that he did not want a Negro to visit his farm who could read, because he would spoil his slaves. After it was known that I was courting the girl, he would not allow me to visit his farm nor any of his slaves to visit ours, but they did visit notwithstanding this order, nearly every Sunday. The girl's aunt was our mutual friend and made all arrangements for our meetings. At one of our secret meetings we decided to elope and fixed March 30, 1864, at nine o'clock, P.M., sharp, as the date for starting.

She met me at the appointed time and place with her entire worldly effects tied up in a handkerchief, and I took her up on the horse behind me. Then in great haste we started for Laclede, about thirty miles north of Brunswick, and the nearest point reached by the Hannibal and St. Joe Railroad. This town was occupied by a squad of Union troops. Having traveled over that country so often, I had acquired an almost perfect knowledge of it, even of the by-paths. We avoided the main road, and made the entire trip without touching the traveled road at any point and without meeting any one and reached Laclede in safety, where we took the train for St. Joe, thence to Weston, where we crossed the Missouri River on a ferry boat to Fort Leavenworth, Kansas. I then felt myself a free man.

I learned soon afterwards that Jesse Boram, Allen Farmer and as many other men as could be hastily gotten together started in pursuit of us, following every road we were supposed to take, and went within six miles of Laclede, hoping to overtake us. Of course they would have ended my earthly career then and there, could they have found me that night. But I had carefully weighed the cost before starting, had nerved myself for action and would have sold my life very dearly had they overtaken us in our flight. How could I have done otherwise in the presence of the girl I loved, one who had forsaken mother, sister and brothers, and had placed herself entirely under my care and protection.

I am satisfied, even now, that I was braver that night than I have ever been since. I was a good shot and knew it, and intended to commence shooting as soon as my pursuers showed up; but it was a Godsend to all concerned, and especially to myself and bride, soon to be, that we were not overtaken; for I was determined to fight it out on that line, as surrender meant death to me. I had buckled around my waist a pair of Colt's revolvers and plenty of ammunition, but I feel now that I could not have held out long before a crowd of such men, and while I might have hit one or two of them, they would in the end have killed me.

My bravery, if that was what affected me, was not of the kind that will not shun danger, for I resorted to every scheme possible to avoid it. We had the start of our pursuers about an hour, or in other words the girl was missed from her room in that time; then it took probably another hour to get the men together. But they stood a very poor show to capture us on the main road, for we left it after the first half mile and took to the brush and by-paths. They expected to overtake us on the main road, where they would have killed me, taken the girl back and given her a severe flogging, but they were badly fooled, for we traveled east, nearly on a straight line for six miles, then turned north, the correct course of our destination.

I had heard it whispered among his Colored people, that Mr. Farmer's house was a kind of rendezvous for the bushwhackers in that part of the country, a place to meet to secure rations, ammunition and information, and that, occasionally, he went out with them at night. If it be true that he acted with bushwhackers, then I assert that he went out with them just once too often, for he was killed as such, during the summer of 1864, while on the run after being halted.

Chapter 5

Turning Points

Chapter Preface

A mong historians, the summer of 1863 represents the traditional turning point of the Civil War. After marching into southern Pennsylvania, Robert E. Lee's Army of Northern Virginia was stopped at the Battle of Gettysburg and turned back, out of Northern territory. Two days after Gettysburg, Union general Ulysses S. Grant captured the fortress town of Vicksburg, Mississippi, after a long siege. The fall of Vicksburg allowed the federal army and navy to seize control of the entire Mississippi River, which, in President Abraham Lincoln's words, now "flowed unvexed to the sea." The loss of the Mississippi valley effectively cut the Confederacy in two—an important part of the overall war strategy decided on by Lincoln and his top commanders.

Yet a crucial military and political point had already been reached that was playing an even more decisive role in the war's outcome. This was the Battle of Sharpsburg, or Antietam, the bloodiest of the entire war, fought in western Maryland in September 1862. The stalemate at Antietam brought the series of early Confederate victories to an end and also stopped Robert E. Lee's threat to Washington, D.C. Sharpsburg proved that, despite their capable officers and spirited men, the Southern army could not overcome the sheer numbers of troops and artillery mustered by the Union side. For the Confederacy, the war became a defensive struggle and a war of attrition that Southerners had much less hope of winning.

More importantly, it was the Battle of Sharpsburg that gave President Lincoln the confidence and the opportunity to deliver the Emancipation Proclamation, freeing the slaves in all territory then in rebellion against the Union. The proclamation, which only affected regions where the federal government could not enforce it, steeled Southern whites with an even greater desire to see the war through to the bitter end. But the people of Europe greeted the proclamation with enthusiasm, robbing the South of a principal hope: that the countries of Europe, especially England and France, would recognize the Confederacy, accept its diplomats, and provide it with a military alliance that would force the Union to negotiate.

Poor Dear Dying Brother!

Frank Perry

On September 7, 1862, General Robert E. Lee brought the Army of Northern Virginia across the Potomac and into Maryland. Lee intended to outmaneuver General McClellan, threaten Washington, D.C., and force the federal government to seek peace terms. The result of this campaign was the Battle of Sharpsburg (or Antietam), which took place on September 17 and turned out to be the bloodiest fight of the entire war.

In this letter to Colonel J. Buchannon, a Georgia soldier named Frank Perry describes the aftermath of the battle and the death of his own brother, Walter Perry.

Martinsburg, Virginia: September 21, 1862

Dear Colonel:

I write to you to let you tell the family that Walter [the writer's brother] was killed at a battle fought at Sharpsburg, Maryland, on Wednesday, 17th instant. On that morning I was standing at the front of the Potomac River opposite Shepherdstown, Virginia, and saw him as he came over. He was lively and gay. He went immediately on to the battlefield and was perhaps half a mile north of the village when ordered to advance. He drew his sword and, waving it in the air, cried, "Come on!" and just at that moment a minié ball [bullet] struck him from the left in the shoulder, which passed through and lodged just under his right arm. That prostrated him and completely paralyzed him from that

Reprinted from a letter of Frank Perry to J. Buchannon, Martinsburg, Virginia, September 21, 1862, as it appears in *"Dear Mother: Don't Grieve About Me. If I Get Killed, I'll Only Be Dead": Letters from Georgia Soldiers in the Civil War,* edited by Mills Lane (Savannah, GA: Beehive Press, 1977).

point to his feet. A friend laid him down and stayed with him until he himself was shot. There they both lay under a terrible fire, the regiment falling back. He was shot three times in the left side. His left leg, just above the ankle, had a minié ball entirely through, leaving a large orifice and his left great toe was shot on top. His cap was shot off his head and torn all to pieces, but did not hit his head. As the enemy had possession of the ground, he was not taken off the battlefield until next day about 2 o'clock. His friends stole in and brought him away.

I went to see about him, and just as I found the regiment they had started with him on a litter to the hospital. When I rode up by his side he opened his eyes and said with energy, "Frank, they got me this time, but I was going ahead like a man." And that he was, said every one of his friends who saw him. It rained a hard rain as we went on. I spread my oil cloth over him and kept him dry. We carried him to a large barn where his brigade and regiment physician had a hospital. He was perfectly conscious and not suffering any pain. We had, however, to cut his clothes off him, as he could not bear his shoulders to be moved. The physician told me as soon as he examined him that there was no hope. Poor, dear, dying Brother! Imagine if you can the agony I then endured. Dr. [   ] gave me two blankets. I laid him on a bed made of clover hay, oil cloth and one blanket, and spread one blanket and took off my own coat—which James Hutchins had dried for me—spread over his shoulders and body. Night soon came and with it darkness. I could not get any candles, and I sat by him, keeping him covered carefully in the darkness, until about 9 o'clock, when I begged a lantern from one of the physicians. In the right place above, I should have stated that I obtained a cup of coffee, of which he drank freely, but could not eat anything. The doctor gave me some brandy, of which I gave him a little occasionally.

At 12 o'clock the doctor came in and told me that our army was falling back to Virginia. The band, who are generally detailed as an ambulance corps, placed him on a litter and we carried him on it to the river about two miles, took him over on a small boat and arrived at Shepherdstown just before day. Our litter was one which had legs and stood up fourteen inches off the ground. We placed it on the sidewalk under a spreading tree, and Colonel Jones of the 22nd Georgia was also wounded and with us, and waited there for the dawning of day, when I took him to a hotel. General Wright was opposite to us, badly wounded, and sent over his aide, Mr. Hazelhurst, with a toddy for Bud. He began to give way about the time we arrived on this side of the river. General Wright's secretary took my horse as soon as we reached the barn with Bud and went over to the wagons to get him some clothes but did not get to me (in consequence of the army retreating across the river he could not get back) until about 9 o'clock the next morning. About daylight or as soon as the people began to move about, every wounded man that could possibly move or be moved went on to Winchester. About 9 o'clock the streets were almost vacant and the Yankees shelling vigorously. Soon rumors came that the

After the horrific Battle of Antietam, the battlefield was littered with wounded and dead soldiers. Some wounded waited days to receive medical attention.

Yankees were crossing the river, and then the last straggler was soon gone, and I was alone except [the] physician.

Watching a Brother Die

Sitting by the dying bedside of the dearest and best of brothers, I resolved to stay with him to the last. Early in [the] morning I met Mave Solomon, who is commanding the Henry Blues, and he detailed one of General Brick Henderson's sons to stay with me. I begged him to go. I had my horse tied at the door and told him that when he was satisfied that he was in immediate danger to take him and make his escape. About this time I asked Bud if he knew he could not live much longer. He says, "I thought as much, Frank, from the first, as you did not tell me that I would ever get well." He then spoke at length very rationally on the subject. He said it was hard for him so young, who had entertained such high hopes of future distinction and usefulness, to lie down and die without even one struggle for life's honors, pleasures and duties. Of home he spoke eloquently, of the bright, golden, glorious hour which he had so often pictured when he should return there. Ah! such eloquence I never before have listened to. He spoke of General Wright's son's future (he had lost one leg at the Manassas fight) and said that he had indulged in some speculations on his sad future, but says he, "Mine is indeed sadder than his, as I am cut off in my youth, just as I put out my hand to reach for the prizes which are awarded to the successful." At first he said that he hoped he was prepared to meet his God in a better world than this, but that he had been a bad, bad, very bad boy. I told him that Christ came to save that very class and that I trusted he would be able to feel that his salvation was sure. He told me that he hoped to meet *us all in Heaven.*

About this time he remarked after speaking again of the sudden termination of his career, "That this is enough to say, don't you think so?" and closed his eyes again. Once more after sitting by some time, watching his breathing grow slower and still slower, that I spoke to him upon the subject and he made this very remark, "Frank, we have talked that

all over and it can't be pleasant to you and it certainly is no
pleasant to me," meaning to speak of his death under the cir
cumstances. Some phases of the care he did not seem to ge
out [of] his mind. He never spoke of any *one* of the famil
but at the end of every few sentences in his remarks woul
say, "Good by, Good by, *Good by to you all*!" He told me t
pay Captain Phillips balance due for his horse and take hin
also to take his watch, &c. The Yankees got his sword bu
did not take his pocketbook nor watch, both of which I have
I have not yet seen his quartermaster but have sent him wor
to take care of his baggage until I can see him. About 1
o'clock I spoke to him again, though he had been going ver
fast for the last hour, and asked him if he knew me. He
opened his eyes and said, "Who, Frank Perry? I think I do
Frank." And then never spoke again.

Arrangements

Precisely at 12 o'clock on Friday, 19th September, his spir
it quietly took its flight to a better world than this. Hender
son and myself shrouded him with a suit of white clothes.
myself closed his eyes and tied a white handkerchief ove
his head. By this time Henderson and myself were the only
men left in the place except citizens. I went out and found
some Bristol Masons [and] consulted with them as to what
course I should pursue. They told me that the enemy cer
tainly would be in the village before I could get him buried
and that when they came I would not be allowed to see him
any more but that I would be taken off and he would be tak
en out and thrown in a grave without a coffin. But that if I
would leave, they as [Masonic] brothers would see that he
was properly buried—that is, as well as the facilities there
and circumstances would admit. They went with me to the
cabinet shop, the proprietor of which was also a brother Ma
son. I paid him for making a coffin and digging the grave,
gave the other brother (whose name I will give you here lest
I may never myself get home out of this war: H.C. Entley,
or his father) Walter's name to have the grave properly
marked, &c. They assured me it would all be as well at-

tended to as though I remained. I went back to where the poor, dear boy lay cold in death, kissed his cold brow and after taking a last long look at his pale yet sweet face, I covered it up again and slowly rode away with the heaviest heart that I have ever carried with me.

It looked to me that I ought to have remained with him and buried him, but under the coloring of things as mentioned above that would perhaps been [foolish of] me and I would have been a captive. I did all that I could do, and it is a great consolation to me, and I know it will be to all of you to know that I was with him in his dying hours to soothe as much as possible his dying spirit. I have written all the particulars, because I know that you will all want to know them. for I may never get home to tell.

I shall write to all in a day or two, and you will then see on what wild goose chase the enemy has been for the last few days. I saw several of the guards but have not been able to hear anything from the others [of] E Company, only that two or three were killed and I did not know them. I hope Asa is all right and that you have all heard from him, as it seems that I cannot hear from him. I sent word to General Wright to take care of Jack until I could get him. I would have given everything in life to have had this bitter cup pass me, but it could not be. Poor, dear boy, he has gone and my heart bleeds twofold when I think of the wailing of the grief-stricken hearts at home when this sad news reaches there, but I can't write more and have written this on the march. Remember me to all and show this letter to my Wife, and I remain truly, &c.

The Death of Stonewall Jackson

Henry Kyd Douglas

> The year 1863 turned out to be the turning point of the Civil War. That spring, under General Lee, the Confederate forces were marching and maneuvering against a Union army commanded by General Joseph "Fighting Joe" Hooker. The Confederates scored an important victory at the Battle of Chancellorsville, which began on May 2nd. Among historians, the battle is best remembered for an astounding flanking maneuver ordered by General Thomas "Stonewall" Jackson, who had first gained renown in the South for his stand at Bull Run in 1861. Jackson's surprise appearance with his corps behind the federal lines turned the tide of the battle at Chancellorsville, but in the hours following the fight he came under "friendly fire" and was mortally wounded.
>
> The last battle and the final hours of Stonewall Jackson are described by Henry Kyd Douglas, a member of Jackson's staff, in his famous memoir *I Rode with Stonewall*.

While at Hamilton's Crossing, the General [Stonewall Jackson] established his Headquarters in tents. His activity did not cease in his efforts to get his corps in condition for the opening of the campaign. After the middle of March we were time and again annoyed and put in motion by rumors of the advance of the enemy, but Hooker really seemed in no hurry.

While at Moss Neck the General began to grant a furlough

Excerpted from *I Rode with Stonewall*, by Henry Kyd Douglas (Chapel Hill: University of North Carolina Press, 1940).

to each of his staff who asked for it. He took no leave himself, and this concession to them was something of a surprise. Once when I was with him I tentatively remarked that I had not been out of the army since I entered it for a day.

"Very good," he broke in, "I hope you will be able to say so after the war is over."

In camp we worked away, some of us to kill time as well as to get the troops in fighting condition and *esprit*. The winter was variable and disagreeable if not severe, and the Stonewall Brigade changed its camp three times. I note that on the 2nd of April I spent a good part of the night in my tent reading [Roman poet] Horace and proving the *pons asinorum* ["bridge of asses"—difficult mathematical problem]. And thus another month passed away.

Little Miss Stonewall

About the 20th of April Mrs. Jackson made a visit to the General with her little daughter, Julia, about five months old, and the General took quarters for them at Mr. Yerby's, perhaps a mile from his camp. This begat more or less social gayety and everybody called on Mrs. Jackson and little Miss Stonewall. Troops would be brought near for parade and review, and the baby would be carried to where they could get a view of her. Mrs. Jackson's attractive looks, manners, and good sense did much to make these visits to her popular and pleasant, and the General was the model of a quiet, well-behaved first father. He was much in evidence, yet he did not seem to neglect any of his official duties.

On the 27th I accompanied the ladies from Corbin Hall, with Captain Stockton Heath, on horseback to call on Mrs. Jackson, and we found quite a gathering of officers and ladies doing the same. I do not forget my embarrassment when at the mischievous suggestion of one of the ladies Mrs. Jackson handed me little Julia to hold for a space. The General walked in and his amusement increased the surrounding merriment, but he made the nurse come to the rescue. Little Julia grew up in her beauty and was very fair to look upon. She married young and died young, and two children take her place with her mother.

But the storm was gathering. At breakfast on the 29th a message from [Confederate] General [Jubal] Early to Jackson told that the enemy were crossing just above Fredericksburg and Jackson's corps began to march toward and past Hamilton's Crossing. Mrs. Jackson and Julia were hurried of to Richmond, and all the decks were cleared for action. I met the General on the road that afternoon and he took me to his quarters to take supper with him. In reply to an enquiry for Mrs. Jackson, he said facetiously he had sent her "to the rear as extra baggage." He was in fine spirits and the prospects of a "scrimmage" seemed to put him in good humor. . . .

Armies on the Move

During the night all orders were issued and preparations made for an early movement the next morning. General Hooker was moving with rapidity and skill. After leaving Sedgwick with a large body of not less than 30,000 to threaten Lee directly from Fredericksburg, the Federal general had crossed some miles above and was concentrating the rest of his large army on our extreme left. He seemed to have no hesitation as to what he intended to do, nor as to the way he was going to do it. He had altogether an army, well-equipped and well-provided, of not less than 125,000 men of all arms, and not less than 400 pieces of artillery. General Lee had nothing like such a force to meet him. Longstreet and D.H. Hill were absent with three divisions, led by such soldiers as John B. Hood, George E. Pickett, and Matt W Ransom. Lee's command of all arms was not over 60,000 with less than 200 guns. But it was observable that neither Lee nor Jackson ever seemed more ready for a fight. Personally, I gave more observation than ever before to the looks of things. During the winter I had been among the ranks and close to them and saw their daily improvement in condition and morale. I had also seen a deal of Lee, Jackson, Hill, Stuart, and others and saw the interest with which they looked upon the steady improvement throughout the army. And now it seemed to me there never had been a better understanding between officers and their troops.

The 1st of May, 1863, was spent principally in getting into position and feeling the position of the enemy. We had moved up to face the advance of Hooker, leaving Early to watch Sedgwick. There had been sufficient skirmishing during the day to indicate clearly that Hooker was on our front in great force and getting ready for a forward movement. But nothing of importance took place that day in the shape of fighting. Both armies spent much of the night throwing up intrenchments.

The night was clear and cold. The General had neither overcoat nor blanket, for his wagon was far in the rear. Lieutenant J.P. Smith, aide-de-camp, offered him his cape, which the General at first refused and then, not to appear inconsiderate of Smith's persistent politeness, accepted. But he did not use it long. Waking up after a short doze, he observed Smith asleep near a tree and went up to him and placed the cape on its owner so quietly that he was not aroused and slept on in comfort. When Smith awoke, the General was asleep in his old position. It was a sad as well as tender incident for the General caught a cold that night, which predisposed his system to that attack of pneumonia which ended in his death.

Stonewall's Finest Maneuver

But neither Lee nor Jackson had any idea of knocking the head of their troops against the breastworks of General Hooker. Major Jed Hotchkiss, Jackson's topographical engineer, had been sent out in the night to ascertain whether there was not a feasible route around the right flank of the enemy. His report with a map satisfied General Lee that it was practicable, and naturally Jackson was selected to make the movement. He then began his last and greatest flank movement; the one that for all time established his reputation—as said by a Federal officer, wounded at Chancellorsville, who had served fifteen years in an European army—as the "supremest flanker and rearer" the world had ever seen.

With General R.E. Rodes's division in front, covered on

the flank and rear by Fitz Lee's cavalry, the column moved
silently and rapidly in a semicircle by Catherine Furnace and
the Brock road, until it came out again on the Plank road
which it had left on the other side of the enemy. Up to thi:

Trouble in Richmond

*More than 100,000 people—job seekers, refugees, pris-
oners, and government workers—crowded into Richmond
after the start of the Civil War. Speculators held back their
goods in hopes of creating scarcity and driving prices
up—and they succeeded. The public's fear and frustration
exploded into a full-scale bread riot on April 2, 1863, just
as the Confederate armies were marching and winning on
the nearby Virginia battlefields. A citizen named H.A.
Tutweiler gave this eyewitness account.*

Thursday morning I went to the office as usual. A few
minutes after I got in, I heard the most tremendous
cheering, went to the window to see what was going on,
but could not tell what it was about. So we all went down
to the street. When we arrived on the scene we found that
a large number of women had broken into two or three
large grocery establishments, & were helping themselves
to hams, middlings [grain by-products], butter and in fact
every kind of eatable they could find. Almost every one of
them were armed. Some had a belt on with a pistol stuck
in each side, others had a large knife, while some were
only armed with a hatchet, axe or hammer. As fast as they
got what they wanted, they walked off with it. The men
instead of trying to put a stop to this shameful proceeding,
cheered them on and assisted them with all in their power. When they found that no one was going to stop them,
they went back & begun to carry off everything they could
lay their hands on, tubs, buckets, brooms, which are selling here for six dollars apiece, hats, shoes, boots, candles,
& various articles too numerous to mention.

William Friedheim, *Freedom's Unfinished Revolution: An Inquiry into the Civil
War and Reconstruction.* New York: The New Press, 1996.

point Jackson had marched about fifteen miles. His first intention was to turn at this point and move down the road against the enemy. But after a brief consultation with General Fitz Lee, he left the Stonewall Brigade with him to prevent any movement down that road and crossing it with the head of his column moved on to the Old Turnpike. He directed me to remain with General Lee and bring in person any report General Lee might wish to send. Thus having completely gained the rear of the Federal right wing, he put his first division in line and moved quickly against the enemy.

From my position with Lee and Paxton on the Plank road in advance of their commands, I witnessed the exciting spectacle. The surprise was complete. There was not even a skirmish line to give General Howard warning that the Rebels were upon him. Having no time for a formation, the retreat became a stampede. It was about six o'clock when the bugles of Rodes—Blackford in charge of them—sounded the advance, while the Eleventh Corps was preparing its evening meal with the sound of whistling and song. Following the bugles were a few scattering shots, then from the opening in the road the whiz of a shell, and, following after the wild game escaping from the wood, "Jackson's Foot Cavalry" were upon them. The grey line moved on regularly with whoop and yell and the rattle of musketry. There was, there could be, no effective attempt at resistance. . . .

The Fatal Volley

Rumors came from the front that the enemy were massing and were getting ready to make a charge down the road from Chancellorsville. General Jackson, determined to investigate for himself, put aside all warnings and rode directly to the front with Boswell, Morrison, and Wilbourn, of his staff, and several couriers and others. Crutchfield was already in the front, locating and directing some artillery. It does not seem likely that the General went directly along the road, but evidently went through our lines at another position. It seems now an unnecessary as well as a fatal thing for him to do. He was soon fired upon by a squad of the enemy and several hors-

es were shot. I believed from what I heard at the time that by
that volley General Jackson was shot through the right hand
Warned that they were actually in the lines of the enemy, the
little cavalcade galloped off to the left and rear, into the shelter of the wood. Suddenly from the rear came a cry of, "Yankee Cavalry!" and a sharp volley [from Confederate guns
rang out on the night air and sent death among its friends.

General Jackson was shot through the left arm below the

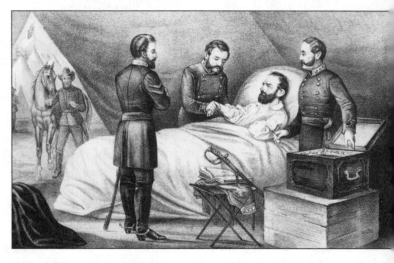

*Men attend to wounded Confederate general "Stonewall" Jackson after the
Battle of Chancellorsville. Although the battle constituted an important victory
for the Confederates, the wounding and eventual death of General Jackson
would prove a terrible difficulty to overcome.*

shoulder, and in the left wrist. Boswell, gallant, chivalric
Boswell, fell from his horse, shot through the heart. Morrison had his horse shot under him. Captain Howard, a staff
officer with Hill, was also wounded. Captain Forbes was
killed and Sergeant Cunliffe mortally wounded. The courier just behind the General was killed, and another wounded; a number of horses were killed or wounded. "Little Sor-
rel" [Jackson's horse] became frantic with fright, rushed first
toward the enemy, then, being turned by the General with
his wounded hand, broke again to the rear. The General was
struck in the face by a hanging limb, his cap was knocked
from his head, and when he was reeling from his saddle his

horse was stopped by Captain Wilbourn into whose arms he fell. Suddenly the enemy's artillery opened on the scene and added to the confusion and horror of it. Others of the party were killed or wounded, and verily, in the language of General Sherman, "war was hell" that night.

Pendleton came and rode rapidly away for a surgeon. McGuire soon came and found that Dr. Barr of Hill's command had been doing what he could for the General. Colonel Crutchfield, Jackson's chief of artillery, had been badly injured by a shot in the leg which disabled him for a year. Captain Benjamin Watkins Leigh, serving that day on Hill's staff, afterwards killed at Gettysburg, had his horse killed and was wounded slightly while helping Smith, who had come up, and Morrison to carry the General to the rear. It was a pandemonium of death and confusion, but above it all rose the iron purpose and commands of Jackson to General Pender and others to hold their positions.

And well was he seconded by Pendleton that night. At first, overcome by his personal grief and loss, as soon as he had seen McGuire and told him what had happened, he fell fainting from his horse. It was but a moment of weakness; he rallied, was soon in the saddle and during the night he remained there, knowing intuitively what should be done. A.P. Hill, having left Jackson when he was started for the hospital, was returning to his division to take command of Jackson's corps and issue orders when he, too, was wounded by a piece of a shell. I was with him at the time and a piece perhaps of the same shell cut through my boot and, cutting my stirrup leather, dropped the stirrup to the ground. . . .

During the greater part of the night the troops were in great disorder, for in spite of the attempt to keep the wounding of Jackson from them it was very generally known throughout the corps. A gloom that was worse than night and disaster seemed to settle upon the army.

A Terrible Premonition

After rendering such assistance as I could to Pendleton in trying to communicate with the parts of the corps, I returned

to General Paxton and the Stonewall Brigade, which had no
been in the confusion that evening. I found General Paxton
very much depressed; he had been so for several days. We
had a long conversation late at night. At the conclusion, he
repeated what he had stated to me in the beginning, that he
was convinced he would not survive the next day's battle
He did not seem morbid or superstitious but he spoke with
earnest conviction. He then told me exactly where certain
private and personal papers were to be found in his desk
then in his headquarter's wagon, and told me what some o
them were. He requested me to see to it that they were no
lost but sent to Lexington. He had the picture of his wife and
his Bible with him. He concluded by asking me to write to
his wife as soon as he was killed and to see that his body
was sent to Lexington by Cox, his faithful orderly, who had
recently been made his aide-de-camp. I was never so im
pressed by a conversation in my life. Paxton was not an
emotional man but one of strong mind, cool action, and
great force of character. He was the last man to give way to
a superstition. When he finished I had no doubt of his sin
cerity and of his awful prescience. Coming upon the horrors
of the evening, I need not say my night was a sleepless
cheerless, vigil.

The next morning was Sunday and we were ordered to be
ready to move forward at daylight. I had at that hour been
along the line of the brigade, and the firing of artillery and
of skirmishers had already begun in other parts of the line
off to our right. I found General Paxton sitting some distance in rear of his line against a tree. He was reading his
Bible. As I approached he closed it, greeted me cheerfully,
and we conversed for a little while on indifferent subjects.
In a short time the order came to get ready to move to the
front. Paxton then recalled our conversation of the night before, asked if I remembered all he had said, and then added
that when he fell, Colonel Funk would be the senior officer
of the brigade and he would doubtless wish me to render
him all the assistance I could in every way. He then said, "I
will go to the right regiments of the Brigade—you look af-

ter the left," and we separated. We did not get into action for some little time.

After a while we became hotly engaged. For some time part of our brigade became separated and I feared Paxton was with it. We soon had some warm work and my time and attention were fully occupied. At the first lull, I was informed that General Paxton had been shot in the first movement and had died almost instantly. Very soon after, Captain R.J. Barton, Assistant Adjutant General, was wounded. I immediately sought Colonel Funk, directed him to take command, and briefly told him what General Paxton had said to me. . . .

"Remember Jackson!"

After this Sunday's fight I rode to the brigade hospital and visited all the wounded. After doing that I went to see General Jackson and was with him for an hour. I found him not only cheerful but talkative—in fact, inquisitive. He seemed to be in excellent condition. He expressed great gratification that General Stuart had handled his corps so admirably. He asked about the positions of the divisions and even of the brigades and what news there was of Early. He asked me to describe as well as I could the movements of the several divisions during the battle and tell him what I knew of the losses.

He then began to enquire about individuals, mentioning a number of officers and asking if they were unhurt. He spoke most feelingly of the deaths of Paxton and Boswell. Then, saying he had heard I had been active with the Old Brigade that day, he asked me to tell him all about its movements. I described to him its different evolutions from the beginning: how Paxton was reading his Bible when the order came to advance, how the brigade assisted in the assault and capture of the first line of the enemy's works, how Paxton was mortally wounded, dying almost immediately, how the brigade then advanced and was repulsed, and how, when Stuart, in person, started it in its last grand charge, it broke over the field toward the enemy, shouting, louder than the din of musketry, "Remember Jackson!" and swept everything like a tempest before it. For a moment his face flushed with excitement and pride and lighted up with the fire of battle. But at once, with moist eyes and quivering voice, he said,

"It was just like them, just like them. They are a noble set of men. The name of Stonewall belongs to that brigade, not to me." This latter sentence he repeated several times before he died. . . .

Sunday, the 10th, was a beautiful day. Service was held by the Reverend Dr. Lacy at General Hill's Headquarters and the text of his sermon was the hopeful one, "We know all things work together for good to them that fear God." It was an imposing service of the deepest solemnity.

Hope was expressed that the General was getting better but private information gave no hope. I find this in my diary, "This afternoon my watch stopped at a quarter past three o'clock. At that moment the heart of Stonewall Jackson ceased to beat, and his soul departed for Heaven."

Stonewall Jackson had performed his greatest achievement and, from the hour he was struck down to the delirium of his last moments, his mind was upon it. He was virtually dying on the field, amid the trophies and ruins of his last victory. His spirit was riding on the whirlwind of the conflict.

"Order A.P. Hill to prepare for action!"

"Pass the infantry to the front—" and his soul seemed ready to go out upon the storm.

And then the light of the eternal future broke upon him and after a pause he said, "No, no, let us cross over the river and rest under the shade of the trees."

That evening the news went abroad, and a great sob swept over the Army of Northern Virginia; it was the heart-break of the Southern Confederacy.

Pickett's Charge at Gettysburg

William C. Oates

The victory at Chancellorsville encouraged Lee to attempt
another invasion of the North in the summer of 1863. This
time, he crossed into Pennsylvania, where the Confederate
army found itself marching towards the small town of Gettysburg on the first day of July. Opposing Lee was a Union army
under the command of General George Gordon Meade. Over
three days, Union and Confederate armies would fight an
immense battle of cavalry charges, infantry maneuvers,
artillery bombardments, trench warfare, and deadly hilltop
skirmishes, all for control of a few farmers' fields around
Gettysburg.

The battle reached its climax on July 3, when 15,000 Confederate troops charged federal troops and guns entrenched
behind a stone wall atop Cemetery Ridge. "Picketts's
Charge," as it has come to be known, turned out to be a costly
failure, representing the high water mark of the Confederacy.
After the Confederate units were thrown back, Lee retreated
from Gettysburg and eventually from Pennsylvania altogether, never again to take the offensive against the stronger
and better supplied Union armies.

Gettysburg and Pickett's Charge are described by Colonel
William C. Oates, a member of the 15th Alabama infantry
regiment who does not hesitate to give his opinions of the
Southern commanders and soldiers and the reasons for their
ultimate failure.

Excerpted from *The War Between the Union and the Confederacy*, by William C. Oates
(New York: Neale, 1905).

The desperate fighting of [July] 2d had accomplished no substantial results. The great question with General Lee was whether to give up the contest on that field and withdraw, or make a further effort. It was a momentous question. If he withdrew it was an acknowledgment, not that he was beaten, but that he had failed to beat Meade, which, the way things are accepted by the world, would be considered a defeat; the purpose of the invasion as having failed, a degree of demoralization would pervade the army, and the people of the entire Confederacy would feel despondent. As a wise commander he would not have ordered the assault, but other considerations urged him to the desperate undertaking. If he made another effort and failed it would be only a defeat, but with a heavy loss of men, and by a desperate effort he might possibly meet with success. But it was a great risk to take. [Confederate General James] Longstreet advised against the third day's attack.

One of the prominent characteristics of General Lee was his boldness and the hazardous moves he many times made. Meade during the night of the 2d strengthened his already strong and almost impregnable position. The disadvantage of Lee's position was that at least a mile of open wheat-field interposed between it and the position held by the Union troops.

To traverse this open space under the fire of massed artillery and a double line of infantry behind a stone wall was too hazardous and success too near impossible. General Longstreet says in his book that he strenuously advised against it and still insisted on turning Meade's left and flanking him out of position. Lee, with all his robust daring and adventurous spirit, should not have ordered the impossible, as was apparent to the skilled observer. But about nightfall of the 2d General [J.E.B.] Stuart reported to his chief. Lee then resolved to try the desperate venture. . . .

Pickett's Charge

In front all the forenoon [of July 3rd] was spent in placing batteries and arranging the charging column, under Longstreet's direction, who was habitually slow; he had no faith in the success of the battle from the first and did not wish to direct this grand assault.

Pickett's division arrived early that morning and were the only fresh troops which had not been engaged. That division belonged to Longstreet's corps and to him was assigned the duty of arranging and conducting the proposed assault. He did not approve it—his heart was not in it. One hundred and fifty guns—more than one-half of all that were in Lee's army—were put in position under the direction of General Alexander, chief of artillery of Longstreet's corps.

A little after 12 o'clock, at a given signal, all these guns opened fire upon the Federals along Cemetery Ridge and were at once replied to by at least an equal number. It was the most powerful cannonade that ever occurred in the world's history of warfare. The ground fairly trembled, the air was sulphurous and full of smoke, caissons were blown up, guns dismounted, horses killed and for two hours the earth was torn in holes by the bursting shells. The bombardment at Toulon in 1793 under young Napoleon was more terrible in its destructiveness, but with less than one-third as many guns.

The Union General Sickles said: "Lee's 200 guns, answered by as many on our side, made but little impression on our lines." The reason was that their infantry were all protected by the stone fence, and earthworks thrown up the night before, and most of their men lay behind the crest of the ridge. Soon after the great battle of the batteries ceased and as the smoke lifted Pickett's division of 5,000 men—fifteen Virginia regiments, formed in column of brigades—supported on the right by Wilcox's five Alabama regiments and on the left by Pender's division of North Carolinians, began a rapid advance against the center of the Union line. The column was at least three-quarters of a mile wide, three lines deep, and contained 15,000 men.

All was silent until this immense column, moving rapidly forward to the assault, came within range of the Federal line, when a terrible artillery fire was opened on the determined men. They were soon in range of the small arms; as men fell the ranks closed up and kept right on. General Sickles said "Longstreet's column advancing toward Cemetery Ridge was torn by our artillery and crushed by the fire of Hancock's infantry and disappeared like ocean waves dashing against a rock-ribbed shore."

When about half the distance had been traversed, without sending any order to Wilcox, Pickett changed his column by the left flank, half a brigade's length, which made a gap between him and Wilcox of about two hundred yards. Why he did this the writer was never able to learn and Wilcox said years afterwards that it was never explained to him. General Longstreet states in his book that it was because the Union line on their right overlapped the Confederate assaulting column. It was a fatal mistake.

General Pickett himself halted at a barn about three hundred yards from the position of the Union troops and remained there until his division was repulsed. This opening exposed Pickett's right flank to the fire of Stanard's Vermont brigade. General Stanard changed front forward on first company of the first battalion and brought his whole brigade in line exactly on the flank of Pickett's column. Wilcox was too hotly engaged in front to turn on Stanard. Pickett's men rushed forward to, and some of them over, the stone fence behind which lay two or three lines of battle. It is called "Pickett's charge" because he commanded the division of direction, but Brigadier-General Armistead, whose brigade was in support, led the charge when near the works and he was killed inside the Union line while holding up his cap on the point of his sword as a guide to his men. That spot is marked by a stone monument with raised letters on it, "High tide of the rebellion." Garnett's brigade came gallantly up to the stone wall and he was killed; Kemper's next, who was wounded and captured. Pickett's column was broken. Trimble, who succeeded General Pender when that officer was killed or mortally wounded in the advance with Pettigrew, came up on a line with Pickett's men, but was shot, from which he lost his leg, and the whole column was repulsed with heavy loss. He was then sixty-five years of age. He lived near thirty years after and died in Baltimore, an utterly unreconstructed rebel, in 1889.

Pickett lost all of his brigadiers and field officers except one major. Only 1,300 of the 5,000 returned from the charge. But I do not wish to be understood as asserting that they were all killed or wounded, for many hundreds of them—a majority—surrendered unhurt. The point assaulted was a very strong one by nature, which had been made still stronger by the engineers and pioneer corps the night before. Meade had double lines of infantry, hundreds of pieces of artillery, strong reserves, and was defended by batteries under the command of able and experienced officers. It was a perfect Gibraltar. The assault was made most gallantly by troops who had never been whipped upon any field and had often won victories against double their number. They had the utmost confidence in General Lee and the officers nearer to them. But no troops can long withstand a heavy fire in front and on the flank at the same time. Had it been otherwise possible for Pickett's column to have bisected Meade's army, that gap between him and Wilcox was fatal. . . .

The Confederates faced severe defeat at the Battle of Gettysburg. Pickett's charge, taking place the third day of the battle, devastated the Confederate troops and left whole regiments wiped out.

Twelve Thousand Flashing Sabres

Without the least prejudice I do believe now and thought so all along through the war, that the men from the Cotton States [Louisiana, Mississippi, Alabama, Georgia, South Carolina, Texas, Arkansas] (and the farther west the more so) were better soldiers and harder fighters than those from the Border States.

The absence of philosophic reason for this apparent difference for a long time puzzled me, but I finally attributed it to the difference between the frontiersman and the citizen of more refined and regular habits of the older States. I therefore believe, having inspected the position since the war, that had [Confederate General John] Hood's division, with him to handle it and fresh as it was before the fight of the previous day, composed as it was of Georgians, Alabamians and Texans (one regiment being from Arkansas) made that charge, with proper supports, notwithstanding the double lines of Union soldiers with heavy reserves behind that stone fence, the position would have been carried and held. But in justice to Pickett's division, it must be admitted that at Gettysburg Hood's was 2,500 men the stronger, two of Pickett's best brigades having been left in Virginia.

General Stuart tried hard to carry out Lee's instructions. He tried to charge into Meade's rear, but the resistance he met with was too great. It was a grand combat which ensued. Years after the battle General Sickles said: "General Stuart's cavalry sent by Lee to assault our rear while the Confederate army attacked in front was driven back by Gregg. Twelve thousand sabres flashing in the July sun, the tread of twelve thousand horses charging over the turf revealed the greatest cavalry combat ever seen on this continent." Many dusty gray and blue young riders, amidst the deadly roar of musketry, the sharp rattle of carbines, the flashing of sabres and the thunders of the artillery, embraced the sleep that knows no waking in this world. Hampton, Stuart's first lieutenant, was seriously wounded and his repulse was complete. Lee was not whipped, but his bold assaults upon Meade's front and rear had been repulsed with heavy losses—it may well be said irreparable ones, yet the morale of that superb army of earnest patriots was still unbroken. Their confidence in the skill of their commander remained unshaken, though he had ordered them to perform an impossibility—they had been repulsed and were torn and bleeding.

The Death of General Farnsworth

On the morning of the 3d of July Law's brigade still constituted the right of the Confederate line and lay along the second foot, up near the abrupt rise on the south side of Big Round Top [one of two adjacent hills to the south of Cemetery Ridge], my regiment [the 15th Alabama] on the right. The old rocks piled up as breastworks still mark the place where the brigade lay. Kilpatrick's Union cavalry were in the woods just on our right flank, which necessitated the extension of a line of pickets for some distance southward and nearly at right angles to our line. Sharp-shooters from the top of the mountain made it a very precarious business for our men to go down to our rear for water. A member of the Fourth Alabama, on picket and acting as a scout on our southern line, overheard in the woods some loud talk between [Union] Generals Kilpatrick and Farnsworth and reported it to General Law at once, by which he was enabled to prepare for what was coining. It seems that Kilpatrick ordered Farnsworth to take a squadron, or battalion of cavalry, and charge through our skirmish line and capture a six-gun North Carolina battery in our rear, Captain Riley, a burly old Irishman, commanding. Farnsworth protested against it until Kilpatrick said, "By God, if you are afraid to go, I will lead the charge myself!" This so piqued Farnsworth, who had but recently been promoted, that he resolved to lead the charge, and did so. He first encountered the First Texas Regiment lying behind a low fence, which was charged over, the Texas regiment having been deployed as skirmishers, and he went for the battery; but the fire from it and a Georgia regiment and a cooking detail on the south caused him to circle around to the west side of the battery, but here he found the Fourth Alabama advancing to meet him. He turned and assailed the battery again, which kept up a constant eruption of grape and canister [shells filled with shrapnel to decimate infantry and cavalry]. His men attacked with their sabres, and a gunner knocked two of them off their horses with a rammer. I had been ordered from the right to move with all possible expedition to the relief of the battery. This I did, rear in front. I did not take time to counter-march, but threw out a few skirmishers as we moved.

We passed through an open space and crossed Plum Run ... and as we rose the ascent in a copse of woods some eight or ten cavalrymen came in between us and the battery. One of its guns just at this moment fired a double charge of canister-shot at the cavalry, which, missing them, came over our heads and through the ranks, making a noise resembling that of the wings of a covey of young partridges, but did us no damage. The officer commanding the cavalry, with pistol in hand, ordered the skirmishers to surrender, to which they replied with a volley. The cavalry commander, his horse, and one of his men fell to the ground, and the others dashed away. Lieutenant Adrian, commanding the skirmishers, with a carbine in hand, advanced and said to the wounded officer, who still grasped his pistol and was trying to rise, notwithstanding he had received three severe and perhaps mortal wounds, "Now you surrender." With an oath he swore he would not do it, and placing his pistol to his own body shot himself through the heart. I halted my regiment and allowed the men to rest where they were. The lieutenant with the skirmishers was Adrian, of the Forty-fourth Alabama Regiment, who was only temporarily with us, having left his own regiment with the carbine, as he said, to try to capture a horse from the cavalry.

I had the facts above related as to the death of Farnsworth stated to me then and there by Adrian, and from what I saw at a distance of not more than fifty steps I am satisfied of their truth. I did not go to the dead man at once, but sat down to rest. One of my skirmishers soon came and said, "Colonel, don't you want that Yankee major's shoulder straps?" holding them up before me. He supposed that the dead man's rank was that of major because he had but one star on each shoulder strap—a single star on the coat collar indicating that rank among the Confederates. I took them and saw at once he was a general, and went to the body. The men were coming up to it in little squads and looking at the dead man in silent amazement on account of Lieutenant Adrian's statement. Upon examination I found letters in his breast-pocket addressed to Gen. E.J. Farnsworth. I read enough to see that one of the letters was from his wife. I then destroyed them to prevent their falling into the hands of irresponsible parties. The monument which has been erected to him of cannon balls is at least one hundred and fifty yards north of where he fell.

A Bad Feeling

A short time after this incident, now late in the afternoon, I was ordered to take up an advanced position in the woods facing east and at right angles to our line at the base of Round Top, but separated from it by a half mile or more southward. The rain, which invariably succeeds a heavy battle, came pouring down. There was a strong line of dismounted cavalrymen within one hundred yards of our front. Night drew on, and I had not received any order. I was there in obedience to an order. The surroundings presented the most weird and lonely appearance. The dead lay scattered through the drear and sombre woods; the fast-scudding clouds overhead shut out all save just enough light, at short intervals, to get a glimpse of the solemn scenes around us. Not a sound was heard; the stillness was awful. I knew, intuitively, that there was something wrong. I felt it, and could not have given any other reason for my apprehension. I started to ride back through the woods toward the place where we had left our comrades, to ascertain the state of affairs. Before I had gone a hundred yards I heard a gun or pistol cap explode a short distance from me. I turned, rode back, and called for Sergt. Wm. R. Holley, of my old company, a brave soldier, but a very cautious, watchful, prudent, and sensible man. (He died at his home in Henry County in 1880.) I told

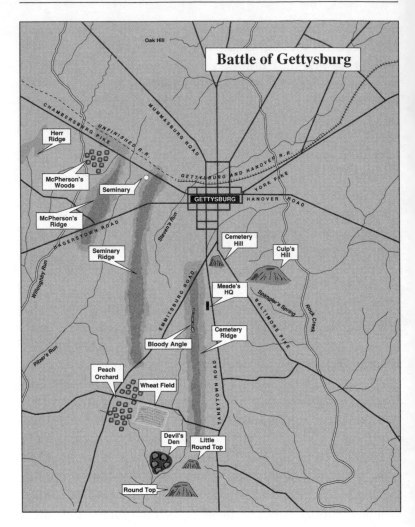

Holley in a low tone what had occurred, and ordered him to creep through the woods, observing everything right and left closely, until he could discover what was there, and then report to me. I rode back a short distance and waited. The leaves were wet, and he glided noiselessly forward; I could not hear him walk. Within a short time Holley returned and reported in his usual broad accent, "A line of Yankees out thar. I went up close to some of them; they are thar sho." I was satisfied of the truth of it. My videtes [scouts] reported the enemy still near, within one hundred yards in front of us.

It was after nightfall, very dark, with Yankees near to us in front and rear. No orders came, and I was satisfied none would come, except from our enemies, and that would be to surrender whenever they found us isolated from the main body of our troops. I resolved to act upon my own judgment, abandon the post without orders, and get out of there. I knew the penalty for disobedience of orders and abandoning my post in the presence of the enemy—it was infamous death if I made a mistake. I was sure of my position, and I took the responsibility, grave as it was. I therefore drew in the videttes from my left and front, faced the regiment to the right, and ordered the men silently to march after me. No man spoke above a whisper nor made any noise. After performing a considerable circuit, the rain pouring down at intervals, we got into the open field and marched westward until we heard troops in our front building breastworks. I did not know which side, but ventured, and to our great relief found our place in the line of Longstreet's corps, and thus escaped from a most perilous situation. We were fortunate, too, in reaching that line at our brigade.

I then learned that late that evening the greater portion of the Union army had been massed to move against Longstreet and crush him, and that just as the movement began General Lee ordered him to retire on a line with Hill's corps, and fortify his position. This the troops were then busily engaged in doing. If any order was ever sent to me to withdraw, I never received it. Colonel Sheffield, of the Forty-eighth Alabama, was commanding the brigade. He said that when the retrograde movement began he sent Tom Sinclaire, brigade courier, with an order to me to withdraw, but the courier was captured and did not reach me. The Union army had advanced, and I was nearly surrounded, and happened to take the only safe retreat. Had I obeyed orders I and all of those with me would have finished our service as prisoners of war, a thing I always dreaded more than the bullets of the enemy.

The next day, July 4, we celebrated by awaiting an attack of the Federals, but they came not. Thus far the Confederates had done all the attacking. They awaited our assaults. Now that they were on their own soil they acted strictly on the defensive, and thereby obtained the advantage of selecting their position. That was just what Longstreet desired Lee to do. But his supplies might soon have been exhausted, and he was too far from his base to readily or easily replenish; hence his defensive policy was annulled by Meade's defensive or waiting policy. Under the circumstances it was masterful in Meade. Lee could not wait; he had to be moving; he could not wait when so far from his base of supplies, and Meade perceived the situation.

As Meade would not assault him in the open field, on the morning of July 5 Lee began his retreat toward the Potomac. There was no hurry, no demoralization. The troops marched slowly, and frequently halted to give time to the wagon-trains and the wounded. The high-tide of the Confederacy had reached its flood. This day began its ebb, which reached low-water mark at Appomattox nearly two years thereafter.

Capture in the Wilderness

Henry E. Handerson

A graduate of Hobart College in Geneva, New York, Henry E. Handerson found a position as a tutor for the family of Washington Compton, a cotton planter of Alexandria, Louisiana, in 1859. When the Civil War broke out, Handerson found that his service in the Confederate army was expected. His diligence and ability came to the attention of his commanders, and eventually Handerson became a staff officer, with a rank and surroundings he found more suitable to his social position.

In May 1864, Handerson and the Confederate army found themselves under attack by General Ulysses S. Grant, the newly promoted overall commander of the Union army. Grant's offensive took his Army of the Potomac directly into a tangled, confusing, and rugged region of Virginia hills and forests known as the Wilderness. The Battle of the Wilderness that followed pitted two desperate and disoriented armies against each other in a fight of smoke, fog, and utter confusion. Handerson describes the actions of his fellow officers during the battle and his capture and imprisonment by the enemy, which put an end to his career as a Confederate soldier.

I had been so busily engaged in the routine duties of my department that I had paid but little attention to the general progress of the great struggle in which we were engaged and was rather surprised than otherwise when on May 4th, 1864, we were ordered to break camp immediately, and

Excerpted from the Civil War memoirs of Henry E. Handerson as they appear under the title of *Yankee in Gray* (Cleveland: Press of Western Reserve University, 1962).

took up once more the well-known route across Mine Run, camping about sundown at Locust Grove or Robertson's Tavern on the Orange and Fredericksburg turnpike [of eastern Virginia]. By sunrise the next morning we were again under arms and ready to move, and I seized the opportunity afforded by some delay in marching, to distribute to the various regiments of my brigade a number of official papers which had come to hand the preceding evening, little thinking that this was the last time I should perform that duty.

It was rumored that the enemy was in front of us, but in what force or with what precise purpose, was not known, at least to the brigade commanders. It was nearly eleven o'clock when we filed into the turnpike, and far down this road the glimmer of a brass field-piece revealed the position of the opposing forces. Advancing along the turnpike to within perhaps half a mile of the supposed position of the enemy, we turned into a woodroad leading off to the left in the direction of Germanna Ford, where we were halted to await orders. After some delay Gen. Stafford became impatient and rode back to endeavor to secure some information as to what he was expected to do, and the men seized the opportunity to take their dinner, smoke, sleep and take such ease as the circumstances admitted.

Under Attack

I was quietly riding along the line, reflecting upon the improvidence of our superior officers in thus marching us up to the enemy without any definite orders, when some of the men who had been out into the dense undergrowth in our front returned hastily with the information that they had seen the skirmishers of the enemy advancing and not more than one hundred yards from our position. I at once called the brigade into line and was preparing to throw out skirmishers along our front, when Gen. Stafford rode up hastily and ordering us to fall back about a hundred yards from the road, formed here a new line of battle and gave the command to "Load." Immediately we advanced through the trees and bushes about a quarter of a mile, when somewhat to our right there burst forth the most tremendous roll of musketry it was ever my fortune to hear. No sound of artillery disturbed this awful roll, which gave no break nor interruption and apparently preserved for at least ten minutes an unwavering intensity. In our immediate front all was quiet save the whistle of an occasional bullet, and the solemnity of the dusky woods resounding with this terrible roll of death, which almost deafened us, and whose effects, though invisible, could readily be imagined by the veteran soldiers of our line, was far more impressive than the excitement of an active struggle.

As we advanced to the crest of a slight elevation, whose further slope was occupied by a small clearing, we were greeted by a hot fire from the enemy's line, which apparently occupied a fringe of woods at the border of the opening. Neither of our flanks was protected, although it was understood that Steuart's brigade was somewhere upon our right and the "Stonewall" brigade [Jackson's brigade carried his nickname even after his death] upon our left, though neither force was visible to us. To charge across this open field without support on either side seemed the acme of rashness, and accordingly we halted and began firing at the enemy in our front. In this position word was brought to me that the Federals were coming in upon our left flank and rear, and putting spurs to my horse I dashed off to the left, where the ride of a few rods [1 rod = 5.5 yards] revealed to me the skirmishers of the hostile line advancing steadily in our rear and almost upon us.

Hastily riding back to Gen. Stafford, I informed him of the situation and received his orders to throw back the left of our line at right angles to the front, so as to face the flanking force and hold them in check if possible. The First Louisiana regiment, consisting of not more than fifty men, was accordingly directed to face to the left and rear, but the Lieut. Col. commanding, instead of coolly and quietly obeying the order, seemed to lose his head entirely, and waving his sword above his head called upon his men to rally around him, which they did in a confused mass, affording little or no protection to our flank and furnishing an excellent target for the enemy. Deployed in a thin line, these men, if coolly handled, might at least have postponed the impending catastrophe, though I could scarcely expect them to entirely check the advance of the hostile force. Seeing no hope of accomplishing anything in the infernal uproar and confusion in this quarter, I rode back to Gen. Stafford and reported, and was then directed by him to ride quickly to the right and endeavor to find the left flank of Steuart's brigade, which should connect with our right.

These were the last words ever heard by me from the unhappy General. Pushing hastily through the undergrowth in the supposed direction of Steuart's brigade, in a few moments I was surprised to almost ride over Capt. Boarman, who was lying upon the ground without arms [weapons] and apparently hiding in the underbrush. To my question what he was doing there, he replied that he had been captured and had escaped, and was hiding from the enemy. I did not at the moment believe him, but feeling that there was not a moment to lose, I rode forward upon my mission as rapidly as the dense undergrowth would permit, shielding my face with one arm from the branches which threatened my eyes. Not five minutes later, as I emerged from a thicket where I was unable to see a rod ahead of me, I was thunderstruck to find myself in front of an advancing line of the enemy and not more than fifty feet from them. I had lost my way and ridden into the very arms of the Federals. The click of a dozen locks and hoarse cries of "Surrender" revealed at once the situation, and a hasty glance convinced me that escape was impossible.

A Prisoner of War

As I threw down my sword in token of surrender I was roughly dragged from my saddle and marched quickly to the rear. Here I was at once disarmed of my pistol and sent in charge of two soldiers to the depot for prisoners near the Wilderness Tavern. On the way thither I was almost pleased to meet the courier of our staff, who had met a fate similar to my own and was likewise being conducted to the same rendezvous. "Misery loves company," and I am sure we greeted each other gladly. It must have been about 4 P.M. when we reached the depot for prisoners, and I was surprised to find here several hundred luckless individuals like myself, who had fallen early victims to the opening struggle. As later arrivals were drawn up in single file in order to take our names, rank, etc., a squad of hangers-on about the camps amused themselves by making witty criticisms of our clothing and personal appearance, which I doubt not would have afforded us ready entrance into the famous ragged regiment of the immortal Falstaff. After enduring this cheap wit for some time I was driven to say: "Boys! Do you think it brave and manly to insult unarmed prisoners? Before long you yourselves may occupy a similar position." Whether this had any effect I cannot say, though several of the men looked rather ashamed and the scurrility soon ceased.

In a short time we were introduced into the prisoners' pen, where, once more to my great surprise, almost the first man I met was Capt. Boarman, who had been recaptured and reached the pen before me. Soon after the Federal provost-marshall made his appearance, and asking for me presented me with a small fly-tent, which under the circumstances was a great convenience and a courtesy which I thoroughly appreciated. Just before sundown the staff-courier, who had been captured with me, and I were again summoned by an officer to Gen. Grant's headquarters, situated near by. On the way thither we learned that the object of our summons was to get from us such information of Gen. Lee's strength, purposes, etc., as we might be able and willing to give, or might let escape us through inadvertence. The courier, with rare thoughtfulness, hastily took from his pocket and tore into fragments the copies of some orders which he had recently served, and when hastily seized by our guard and handled rather roughly for his prudence, I applauded his faithfulness and protested strongly against his abuse. It would have been wiser had I imitated his thoughtfulness, for on finishing a thorough search of the courier, the guard, under orders of their officer, set at once to work to search me, in spite of my protestations against such an indignity. In my pockets were found some orders of the preceding day relating to details of drill, etc., and which I had forgotten to destroy. They were of no importance whatever, except, perhaps as revealing the number of regiments in Stafford's brigade and the names of the commanding officers, but I was greatly mortified at my carelessness in neglecting to destroy them. These papers, with the fragments of the courier's orders, were conveyed to the tent of Gen. Grant, where some sort of a council seemed to be in progress. I do not recollect, however, that any further examination of us was made, and about dusk we were reconducted to the prison-pen, where we spent our first night as prisoners-of-war.

Marching to the Rear

The following morning we were marched a short distance further to the rear, where we bivouacked, listening anxiously to the continued roar of musketry which told of the fierce conflict progressing in our front, and animated with hope or depressed with sorrow as the sounds of battle seemed to approach or recede.

About sundown the sharp rattle of musketry toward the Federal right, the appearance of soldiers running rapidly to the rear and the stampede of the trains in our vicinity raised us to the pinnacle of hope, and hastily snatching up our little baggage, we prepared for the deliverance which seemed now at hand. In a few moments, however, we were ordered to move from our present position, and under a strong guard took in the darkness the road toward Chancellorsville. The obscurity of the night and the forest offered abundant opportunity to individuals to escape, but the labyrinths of the Wilderness were too tangled and winding to present much hope of permanent success in avoiding the masses of the enemy by whom we were surrounded.

The next day we continued our march towards Fredericksburg, passing the Negro troops of [Union General Ambrose] Burnside, who gazed upon us with as much curiosity as hatred as we filed through their midst. Some of our guards had tried to frighten us by stories of the probable actions of this Negro corps when they saw us, intimating that it was extremely likely that they would massacre us on sight. I cannot say, however, that we felt greatly alarmed, and the Negroes in fact offered us little, if any, more insult than their white companions had done before. For the most part we simply eyed each other with mutual curiosity and dislike. As we progressed towards Fredericksburg our ranks were constantly augmented by new arrivals of prisoners, so that we were able to keep ourselves fairly well informed of the progress of the struggle. The body of Gen. Sedgwick, killed before Spottsylvania, was borne by us on Monday the 9th, and bore silent witness that the misfortunes of war were by no means entirely on the Confederate side.

On the 13th a large body of prisoners, chiefly from Johnson's division, joined us, and from them I learned of Gen. Stafford's death from a wound received about the time of my capture. He had been shot through the body, and survived only about 24 hours in great agony. Yet he was said to have asked many questions about me, and to have expressed many apprehensions as to my fate. Indeed it was reported that I had been seen to fall wounded on the battlefield of the 5th. Poor Stafford! A braver man never lived! His friendship for me was always a mystery, since our education and natural dispositions were as diverse as possible. But in good or evil report he was alike my firm and trusty friend, whose support could always be counted upon in positions of doubt and anxiety. He died as he would have chosen, on the field of battle with his face to the foe. May his soul rest in peace!

Fort Delaware

From the vicinity of the Wilderness we were conducted to Fredericksburg, where we took the cars to Acquia Creek and were then embarked on steamers for Fort Delaware in the Delaware river, some thirty miles below Philadelphia. We reached the fort about May 17th, 1864, and officers and men were then separated and assigned to different barracks. The latter consisted of simple wooden houses, around the interior of which wooden platforms in two tiers, like the berths of a steamer, were erected to serve as beds. The barracks were reasonably clean, and to men accustomed to the hardships of active service the hard planks of these "bunks" formed a sumptuous resting-place. Our meals were served in a long building standing by itself within the enclosure and known as the "dining-room." They consisted ordinarily of bread and coffee for breakfast, bread and meat for dinner and plain bread for supper. The food was of good quality and sufficient in quantity, and though, of course, not always tempting to a fickle appetite, was yet quite as good as the average ration of the Confederate army. The military prison was under the command of Brig. Gen'l Schoepf, and was, on the whole, well conducted and humanely administered.

The leisure of the prisoners was occupied in reading, games, puzzles, etc., and after a short sojourn in my new quarters I organized a class in Latin and Greek, which afforded me congenial occupation and prevented idle repinings at my enforced quietude. Soon after my arrival at Fort Delaware I wrote to Mr. E.W. Palmer of Cleveland, asking him to lend me a small sum of money for my immediate necessities, and was surprised to receive a reply from my father, who had been driven out of Tennessee by the hardships of the war in that neighborhood, and had returned a few months before to his old home in Cleveland. For three months the monotony of prison life was undisturbed by any events of importance, and rest with sufficient food had restored my strength and spirits. We were permitted to know little of the results of the campaign in progress, though enough was gleaned from contraband newspapers and chats with our guards to convince us that it had been unprecedentedly bloody and quite indecisive.

The Immortal Six Hundred

On August 13th, however, an officer appeared in the barracks and calling a roll of some 600 Confederate officers, directed them to prepare for immediate departure. My name appeared upon this roll, and full of excitement I hastily packed up my few impedimenta [baggage] and made ready to leave my quarters. The object of our removal was not stated in the order which directed its preparation, and the wildest rumors and speculations spread throughout the barracks. We were to be exchanged at once on arriving at Fortress Monroe; we were selected as victims of retaliation for certain alleged inhumanities of the Confederate authorities; we were to be simply removed to another prison, etc. All these theories were discussed over our pipes, and accepted and rejected in accordance with the varying proclivities of the hearers. Nothing, however, was known as to the real object of our removal, and with the utmost curiosity we awaited the result.

On August 20th we embarked upon the S.S. Crescent City, in the hold of which we were provided with shallow wooden "bunks," and nearly suffocated with heat and foul air. The officers of the guard, however, allowed us as much liberty in coming upon deck as was consistent with safety, and, indeed, treated us with great humanity. Fortunately the weather was fair and the sea smooth, and our ocean trip uneventful, save a narrow escape from shipwreck occasioned by the steamer running in too close to the coast and grounding off Cape Romaine on the Carolina coast. A conspiracy to overpower our guards, seize the steamer and run for the Bermudas was hatching when this accident occurred, but the resulting excitement and uncertainty as to the fate of the steamer and our own safety from immediate destruction disconcerted the plot for the moment, and the appearance of a U.S. gunboat soon after on the lookout for us put an end to all hope of success. Fortunately, after several hours' delay, the steamer succeeded in extricating herself from her dangerous position, and we proceeded to Hilton Head, reaching there on August 25th. Here we remained on shipboard, and on September 1st again moved up to Charleston harbor, which we reached the same day.

Chapter 6

The Death of the Confederacy

Chapter Preface

From their commander's tents, Robert E. Lee and Ulysses S. Grant plotted marches and countermarches through the mountains and forests of Virginia during the bloody summer of 1864. The two armies fought major battles at the Wilderness, at Spotsylvania Court House, and at Cold Harbor. In June, after a failed attack on Petersburg, which lay south of Richmond, the two armies dug entrenchments and prepared for a siege. Two weeks later a Confederate cavalry force under Jubal Early mounted a raid through Maryland and into the District of Columbia, in sight of the Capitol dome, but it was turned back while President Abraham Lincoln watched the fighting from the parapets of Fort Stevens. Early's daring raid and the skillful maneuvering of the Army of Northern Virginia could not disguise a crucial fact: The Confederacy was slowly but certainly retreating, down the Virginia roads towards its capital of Richmond, where at some point it would have to make a last stand or surrender.

Although the Union was losing more men, the South was losing men that it could not replace. Arms, ammunition, food, and clothing all grew scarce. Union general Philip Sheridan ravaged the Shenandoah Valley, while Union general William Sherman's destructive march through Georgia, and then through the Carolinas, deprived the South of vital productive land and nearly served to break Southern morale altogether.

Another blow came with the reelection of President Lincoln in November 1864. Lincoln vowed to see the war through to final victory, and the people of the North had voted their enthusiastic support. A stubborn overconfidence prevented President Jefferson Davis from asking for terms for peace, although he did allow his vice president, Alexander Stephens, to meet with Lincoln at Hampton Roads, Virginia, in February 1865. Stephens insisted on negotiating for an independent Confederacy, but Lincoln refused. The Confederate leaders doomed their cause to an abject military surrender, carried out by their finest officer, at Appomattox Courthouse, Virginia, in April 1865.

On the Picket Line at Chattanooga

Joseph Polley

Despite the dangers of war, soldiering often provided the fighting men of the Confederacy with excitement and amusement, as seen in the letters of Joseph Polley. A member of the Texas Brigade, Polley took part in the bitter fighting around Chattanooga, Tennessee in late 1863, which eventually forced the Confederate army on a disastrous retreat through northern Georgia. Polley describes a watchful night on picket duty, where Union and Confederate soldiers observed a certain code of honor while exchanging jibes as well as bullets.

I was lucky enough to be on picket duty a few nights ago with my friends Will Burges and John West, of Companies D and E of the Fourth, each of whom is not only a good soldier, but a most entertaining companion. As the night advanced, it became cold enough to make a fire very acceptable, and, appropriating a whole one to ourselves, we had wandered from a discussion of the war and of this particular campaign that was little flattering to [commander of the Confederate forces around Chattanooga] General [Braxton] Bragg, into pleasant reminiscences of our homes and loved ones, when someone on horseback said, "Good evening, gentlemen." Looking hastily up, we discovered that the intruder was General Jenkins, alone and unattended by either aide or orderly, and were about to rise and salute in approved military style, when, with a smile plainly percepti-

Excerpted from *A Soldier's Letters to Charming Nellie*, by J.B. Polley (New York: Neale, 1908).

ble in the bright moonlight, he said, "No, don't trouble your-selves," and, letting the reins drop on his horse's neck, threw one leg around the pommel of his saddle and entered into conversation with us.

Had you been listening for the next half hour or so, Charming Nellie, you would never have been able to guess which of us was the General, for, ignoring his rank as com-pletely as we careless Texans forgot it, he became at once as private a soldier as either of us, and talked and laughed as merrily and unconcernedly as if it were not war times. I offered him the use of my pipe and smoking tobacco, Burges was equally generous with the plug he kept for chewing, and West was even polite enough to regret that the whisky he was in the habit of carrying as a preventive against snake bites was just out; in short, we were beginning to believe General Jenkins of South Carolina the only real general in the Confederate service, when, to our surprise and dismay, he straightened himself up on his saddle, and climb-ing from "gay to grave, from lively to severe," announced that at midnight the picket line would be expected to ad-vance and drive the Yankees to the other side of the creek.

We might easily have forgiven him for being the bearer of this discomforting intelligence had that been the sum total of his offending; but it was not; he rode away without expressing the least pleasure at having made our acquaintance, or even of-fering to shake hands with us—the necessary and inevitable consequence of such discourtesy being that he descended at once in our estimation to the level of any other general.

Imperative Action

But midnight was too near at hand to waste time in nursing indignation. Instant action was imperative, and resolving ourselves into a council of war with plenary powers, it was unanimously decided by the three privates there assembled that our recent guest was an upstart wholly undeserving of confidence; that the contemplated movement was not only foolish and impracticable, but bound to be dangerous; and that, if a single shot were fired at us by the enemy, we three

would just lie down and let General Jenkins of South Carolina do his own advancing and driving. Being veterans, we
knew far better than he how easy it was at night for opposing lines to intermingle with each other and men to mistake
friends for enemies, and we did not propose to sanction the
taking of such chances.

*A sharpshooter sits on picket duty, waiting for the enemy. Picket duty was
considered a desirable job for a soldier.*

All too soon the dreaded and fateful hour arrived; all too
soon the whispered order "Forward" was passed from man
to man down the long line, and, like spectral forms in the
ghastly moonlight, the Confederate pickets moved slowly
out into the open field in their front, every moment expecting to see the flash of a gun and hear or feel its messenger
of death, and all awed by the fear the bravest men feel when
confronting unknown danger. Not ten minutes before, the
shadowy forms of the enemy had been seen by our videttes
[scouts], and if the line of the creek was worth capturing by
us, it surely was worth holding by the Yankees. But all was
silent and still; no sight of foe, no tread of stealthy footstep,
no sharp click of gunlock—not even the rustling of a leaf or
the snap of a twig came out of the darkness to relieve our

suspense and quiet the expectant throbbing of our hearts.

Under these circumstances, West, Burges, and your humble servant, like the brave and true men they are, held themselves erect and advanced side by side with their gallant comrades until the terra incognita and impenetrability of the narrow but timbered valley of the stream suggested ambush and the advisability of rifle-pits [small trenches]. Working at these with a will born of emergency, we managed to complete them just as the day dawned, and jumping into them with a sigh of inexpressible relief—our courage rising as the night fled—waited for hostilities to begin. But the Yankees had outwitted us, their withdrawal, by some strange coincidence, having been practically simultaneous with our advance—they taking just enough start, however, to keep well out of our sight and hearing. West remarked next morning, "It's better to be born lucky than rich," but whether he referred to our narrow escape, or to that of the Yankees, he refused to say. . . . Soon afterward a truce along the picket lines in front of the Texans was arranged; that is, there was to be no more shooting at each other's pickets—the little killing and wounding done by the practice never compensating for the powder and shot expended, and the discomfort of being always on the alert, night and day.

Them D—d Secessionists

But the South Carolinians, whose picket line began at our left, their first rifle-pit being within fifty feet of the last one of the First Texas, could make no terms, whatever. The Federals charge them with being the instigators and beginners of the war, and, as I am informed, always exclude them from the benefit of truces between the pickets. It is certainly an odd spectacle to see the Carolinians hiding in their rifle pits and not daring to show their heads, while, not fifty feet away, the Texans sit on the ground playing poker, in plain view and within a hundred yards of the Yankees. Worse than all, the palmetto fellows [South Carolinians] are not even permitted to visit us in daylight, except in disguise—their new uniforms of gray always betraying them wherever they

go. One of them who is not only very fond of, but successful at, the game of poker, concluded the other day to risk being shot for the chance of winning the money of the First
Texas, and, divesting himself of his coat, slipped over to the
Texas pit an hour before daylight, and by sunrise was giving his whole mind to the noble pastime.

An hour later a keen-sighted Yankee sang out, "Say, you
Texas Johnnies! ain't that fellow playing cards, with his
back to a sapling, one of them d—d South Carolina secessionists? Seems to me his breeches are newer 'n they ought
to be." This direct appeal for information placed the Texans
between the horns of a dilemma; hospitality demanded the
protection of their guest—prudence, the observance of good
faith toward the Yankees. The delay in answering obviated
the necessity for it by confirming the inquirer's suspicions,
and, exclaiming, "D—n him, I just know it is!" he raised his
gun quickly and fired. The South Carolinian was too active,
though; at the very first movement of the Yankee, he sprang
ten feet and disappeared into a gulch that protected him
from further assault . . . .

The Inveterate Straggler

Jack Smith, of Company D, is sui generis [one of a kind]. A
brave and gallant soldier he is yet an inveterate straggler,
and is therefore, not always on hand when the battle is raging, but at Chickamauga he was, and, singularly enough,
counted for two.

Another member of Company D is constitutionally opposed to offering his body for sacrifice on the altar of his
country, and, when he cannot get on a detail which will keep
him out of danger, is sure to fall alarmingly sick. Jack determined to put a stop to this shirking, so early on the morning of the 19th, he took the fellow under his own protecting
and stimulating care, and, attacking him in the most vul-
nerable point, to the surprise of everybody, carried him into
and through the fight of that day.

"Come right along with me, Fred, and don't be scared a
particle," Jack was heard to say in his coaxing, mellifluous

voice as we began to advance on the enemy, "for I'll shoot the head off the first man who points a gun in front of you, and I'll watch out for your carcass, and after we have whipped the Yanks you an' me'll finish them bitters in my haversack."

"But I don't like bitters," protested Fred in a trembling voice.

"I know that, ole feller, an' I don't generally like 'em myself, but these are made on the old nigger's plan—the least mite in the world of cherry bark, still less of dogwood, and then fill up the bottle with whisky."

Needless to say that after the battle was over and Jack had brought his protege safely through its perils, quite a number of comrades looked longingly at the bottle. In vain, however; Jack was loyal to his promise and he and Fred were the merriest men in Company D that night.

Bread Riots and Kindred Amenities

John B. Jones

As the Union forces closed in on Richmond in the spring of
1865, the people of the Confederacy suffered hunger, fear,
and increasing desperation. Resentment toward speculators,
who were attempting to profit from the worsening food shortages, exploded into riots in the streets of the capital. While
President Davis attempted to calm the restless civilians, his
outnumbered generals maneuvered for some kind of advantage in the battlefield.

The darkest days of the Confederacy were at hand. John B.
Jones, a government clerk living in Richmond at the time,
witnessed the actions of civilians, soldiers, and politicians
while worrying over preparations for his own family and their
uncertain future.

March 27th.—This is the day appointed by the President
[Jefferson Davis] for fasting and prayers. Fasting in
the midst of famine! May God save this people! The day
will be observed throughout the Confederacy.

Mr. G.W. Randolph was the counsel of the speculators
whose flour was impressed [seized], and yet this *man,* when
Secretary of War, ordered similar impressments repeatedly.
"Oh, man! dressed in a little brief authority," etc.

Mr. Foote has brought forward a bill to prevent trading
with the enemy. Col. Lay even gets his pipes from the enemy's country. Let Mr. Foote smoke that!

Excerpted from diary entries of John B. Jones as they appear in *A Rebel War Clerk's Diary,* edited by Earl Schenck Miers (New York: Sagamore Press, 1958).

March 28th.—We have nothing additional or confirmatory from the West. A letter from Gen. Beauregard states that he has but 17,000 men in South Carolina, and 10,000 in Georgia, 27,000 in all. He asks more, as he will be assailed, probably, by 100,000 Federals. The President refers this important letter to the Secretary of War, simply with the indorsement, "this is an exact statement of affairs in South Carolina and Georgia."

Col. Lay predicts that we shall be beaten in thirty days, or else we shall then be in the way of beating the enemy. A safe prediction—but what is his belief? This deponent saith not. There will be fearful odds against us, and yet our men in the field fear nothing.

We are sending Napoleons [artillery pieces] up to Lee. But the weather, which has been fine for the last two days, is wet again. If Hooker makes a premature advance, he will be sure to "march back again."

March 29th.—No news. Yet a universal expectation. What is expected is not clearly defined. Those who are making money rapidly no doubt desire a prolongation of the war, irrespective of political consequences. But the people, the majority in the United States, seem to have lost their power. And their representatives in Congress are completely subordinated by the Executive, and rendered subservient to his will. President Lincoln can have any measure adopted or any measure defeated, at pleasure. Such is the irresistible power of enormous executive patronage. He may extend the sessions or terminate them, and so, all power, for the time being, reposes in the hands of the President.

Everything depends upon the issues of the present campaign, and upon them it may be bootless to speculate. No one may foretell the fortunes of war—I mean where victory will ultimately perch in this frightful struggle. We are environed and invaded by not less than 600,000 men in arms, and we have not in the field more than 250,000 to oppose them. But we have the advantage of occupying the interior position, always affording superior facilities for concentration. Besides, our men *must* prevail in combat, or lose their property, country, freedom, everything,—at least this is their conviction. On the other hand, the enemy, in yielding the contest, may retire into their own country, and possess everything they enjoyed before the war began. Hence it may be confidently believed that in all the battles of this spring, when the numbers are nearly equal, the Confederates will be the victors, and even when the enemy have superior numbers, the armies of the South will fight with Roman desperation. The conflict will be appalling and sanguinary beyond example, provided the invader stand up to it. That much is certain. And if our armies are overthrown, we may be no nearer peace than before. The paper money would be valueless, and the large fortunes accumulated by the speculators, turning to dust and ashes on their lips, might engender a new exasperation, resulting in a regenerated patriotism and a universal determination to achieve independence or die in the attempt. . . .

Six Months of Winter

March 30th.—The gaunt form of wretched famine still approaches with rapid strides. Meal is now selling at $12 per bushel, and potatoes at $16. Meats have almost disappeared from the market, and none but the opulent can afford to pay $3.50 per pound for butter. *Greens,* however, of various kinds, are coming in; and as the season advances, we may expect a diminution of prices. It is strange that on the 30th of March, even in the "sunny South," the fruit-trees are as bare of blossoms and foliage as at mid-winter. We shall have fire until the middle of May,—six months of winter!

I am spading up my little garden, and hope to raise a few vegetables to eke out a miserable subsistence for my family. My daughter Ann reads Shakespeare to me o' nights, which saves my eyes.

March 31st.—Another stride of the grim specter, and cornmeal is selling for $17 per bushel. Coal at $20.50 per ton, and wood at $30 per cord. And at these prices one has to wait several days to get either. Common tallow candles are selling at $4 per pound. I see that some furnished houses are now advertised for rent; and I hope that all the population that can get away, and subsist elsewhere, will leave the city.

The lower house of Congress has passed a most enormous tax bill, which I apprehend cannot be enforced, if it becomes a law. It will close half the shops—but that may be beneficial, as thousands have rushed into trade and become extortioners.

I see some batteries of light artillery going toward Petersburg. This is to be used against the enemy when he advances in that direction from Suffolk. No doubt another attempt will be made to capture Richmond. But Lee knows the programme, I doubt not.

Bread Riots

April 2d.—This morning early a few hundred women and boys met as by concert in the Capitol Square, saying they were hungry, and must have food. The number continued to swell until there were more than a thousand. But few men were among them and these were mostly foreign residents, with exemptions in their pockets. About nine A.M. the mob emerged from the western gates of the square, and proceeded down Ninth Street, passing the War Department, and crossing Main Street, increasing in magnitude at every step, but preserving silence and (so far) good order. Not knowing the meaning of such a procession, I asked a pale boy where they were going. A young woman, seemingly emaciated, but yet with a smile, answered that they were going to find something to eat. I could not, for the life of me, refrain from expressing the hope that they might be successful; and I remarked they were going in the right direction to find plenty in the hands of the extortioners. I did not follow, to see what they did; but I learned an hour after that they marched through Cary Street, and entered diverse stores of the speculators, which they proceeded to empty of their contents. They impressed all the carts and drays in the street, which were speedily laden with meal, flour, shoes, etc. I did not learn whither these were driven; but probably they were rescued from those in charge of them. Nevertheless, an immense amount of provisions, and other articles, were borne by the mob, which continued to increase in numbers. An eye-witness says he saw a boy come out of a store with a hat full of money (notes); and I learned that when the mob turned up into Main Street, when all the shops were by this time closed, they broke in the plate-glass windows, demanding silks, jewelry, etc. Here they were incited to pillage valuables, not necessary for subsistence, by the class of residents (aliens) exempted from military duty by Judge Campbell, Assistant Secretary of War, in contravention of Judge Meredith's decision. Thus the work of spoliation went on, until the military appeared upon the scene, summoned by Gov. Letcher, whose term of service is near its close. He had the Riot Act read (by the mayor), and then threatened to fire on the mob. He gave them five minutes' time to disperse in, threatening to use military force (the city battalion being present) if they did not comply with the demand. The timid women fell back, and a pause was put to the devastation, though but few believed he would venture to put his threat in execution. If he had done so, he would have been hung, no doubt.

About this time the President appeared, and ascending a dray, spoke to the people. He urged them to return to their homes, so that the bayonets there menacing them might be sent against the common enemy. He told them that such acts would bring *famine* upon them in the only form which could not be provided against, as it would deter people from bringing food to the city. He said he was willing to share his last loaf with the suffering people (his best horse had been stolen the night before), and he trusted we would all bear our privations with fortitude, and continue unified against the Northern invaders, who were the authors of all our sufferings. He seemed deeply moved; and indeed it was a frightful spectacle, and perhaps an ominous one, if the government does not remove some of the quartermasters who have contributed very much to bring about the evil of scarcity. I mean those who have allowed transportation to forestallers and extortioners.

Gen. Elzey and Gen. Winder waited upon the Secretary of War in the morning, asking permission to call the troops from the camps near the city, to suppress the women and children by a summary process. But Mr. Seddon hesitated, and then declined authorizing any such absurdity. He said it was a municipal or State duty, and therefore he would not take the responsibility of interfering in the matter. Even in the moment of aspen consternation, he was still the politician. I have not heard of any injuries sustained by the women and children. Nor have I heard how many stores the mob visited; and it must have been many.

The Siege of Petersburg

Charles Blackford

> After driving through and around the Confederate army in the
> spring and summer of 1864, General Grant arrived at Peters-
> burg, Virginia, a crucial rail junction lying south of Rich-
> mond. Cutting off and capturing Petersburg, Grant knew,
> would sever the capital's lifeline, eventually force General
> Lee to abandon the city and end the war. Also realizing these
> facts, Lee put up a stiff resistance, arranging the Army of
> Northern Virginia into heavily fortified positions. The siege
> of Petersburg would last through the winter and into early
> 1865 and, as Grant predicted, the city's fall would bring the
> war to a swift end.
>
> In his letters home to his wife, Captain Charles Blackford
> describes the early days of the siege of Petersburg, rising
> prices in Richmond, and a failed attack by the Union army on
> the formidable Confederate defenses.

July 11th. We are camped just outside of town. Not
enough change of any sort since my last, except possibly, the dust is thicker, the grass more parched and the sun
hotter. The whole country around here is filled with refugees
from Petersburg in any kind of shelter, many in tents. . . .
Every yard for miles around here is filled with tents and little shelters made of pine boards, in which whole families
are packed; many of these people of some means and all of
great respectability. There must be much suffering. Thus far,

Excerpted from *Letters from Lee's Army*, edited by Charles Minor Blackford III (New York: Scribner, 1947).

while the shelling has done much harm to houses and property, only one *soldier* has been wounded and none killed. Some five or six women have been killed and as many wounded, most of whom were negroes. And this is all they have done. Yesterday, about the time they thought the people were going to church, they commenced a tremendous cannonade, as if with the hope of killing women and children en route to church.

The sinking of the Alabama [the successful Confederate raiding cruiser] gives us great concern, and we are very anxious to hear from [Confederate General Jubal] Early [who was conducting a successful drive on Washington, D.C.]. I fear he has undertaken more than he can do with his small force, and he is likely to come to grief. . . .

Much Unfavorable Comment

July 17th. No news, and no movement except the incessant shelling and the constant ring of the rifles of the sharpshooters on the lines. Last night, about eleven some five or six mighty siege guns were fired, which made the most terrific sound I ever heard. Early has withdrawn from near Washington.

I have taken cold and have a headache and fever. I believe the terrible dust has much to do with it and the hard fare. I can get little or nothing to eat, the best is blue-looking beef and the terrible bread cooked in camp. We have no coffee, tea or sugar. There is much unfavorable comment in the army about [Confederate General Joe] Johnston's constant retreats. Lee would have fought Sherman at Dalton. It is said [Confederate General John B.] Hood is to relieve him. Hood is not the man for such a place. [Confederate General James] Longstreet would be better. Johnston's army has been taught that falling back is the aim of a campaign and that fighting is an incident. Lee has taught us that an occasional retrograde movement is an incident and fighting is the aim. There have been more desertions of late than ever before. I hear that even some Virginians have deserted to the enemy. The hard lives they lead and a certain degree of hopelessness which is stealing over the conviction of the best and bravest will have some effect in inducing demoralization hitherto unknown.

The Richmond papers give me great anxiety. There is a shadow in them of a defeat of Early in the [Shenandoah] Valley. It is only a rumor, but I find bad rumors are always true while good ones are often false. My cold seems touching my vitals. I cannot see, hear or smell, and, but for you and Nannie, would as soon be dead as alive. Grant is making some move. He is taking troops to the north side of the James River, and as a consequence Kershaw's division moves today. There is a rumor Grant is dead. I do not believe it, but it would make little difference to us. He is a hard fighter but no match for Lee as a commander of an army.

July 27th. I went to Richmond day before yesterday on business. Not satisfactory as almost all I wanted to see were out of town. I took breakfast with Col. Robert L. Owen, president of the Virginia and Tennessee Railroad. His bill was $141 for three but it was elegant. It was at Tom Griffin's. It was the best meal I have had for two years. I am glad that he, not me, had to pay the bill. News from Early is encouraging.

The schedule of prices fixed by the commission shocked me beyond measure and it is hard to believe they were such fools. I take that view because it is more charitable than calling them knaves. It is, as the Albemarle farmer would say, an official acknowledgment of bankruptcy, and is a deathblow to the currency. It carries starvation to the non-producers for the market price of everything to eat is far higher than those fixed by the commissioners. If they put wheat at $30 a bushel the farmers will at once charge the starving consumers $120. How are our people to live? The soldiers' wives and families? How are you and Nannie to live? It is a fearful question. The non-producer has nothing to sell, and one can make no money even if not in the army; and what can a soldier do at seventeen dollars a month in Confederate money? The producer has everything. He is exempted from military service if a large producer because [of what] he is. He exchanges his corn and wheat for coffee and sugar, prates about the hardships of war and the high prices, buys nothing and complacently asks the starving wife of his friend who is in the army $100 a bushel for wheat, $4 a quart for tomatoes, and if he does not get it he locks the wheat up for higher prices and feeds the tomatoes to the hogs. You and mother are suffering from this now. This does not apply to the farmers of Orange, Culpeper, Fauquier, Loudoun and the Valley whom the enemy have robbed so heavily. They are as liberal as they are brave and valiant.

War Is a Sad Thing

Camp near Drewry's Bluff, July 31st. I am down here on duty with Pickett's division. There is much activity but I do not know what it is. Reports reached us last night of quite a severe attack at Petersburg on yesterday morning. Grant's mining operations [digging under Confederate lines and filling the tunnels with explosives] culminated there in blowing up one of our batteries, by which twenty-one men and three guns were disabled. An assault on the breach was at once made with negro troops who, report says, carried the fort in spite of Hayward's South Carolina brigade. This is the story, whether true or not you will know long before this reaches you. We certainly hold our old line, and the enemy took nothing by his attack but a severe repulse. Grant had moved three corps to the north side and General Lee followed with three divisions. Yesterday morning they had all disappeared and the mine exploded at Petersburg, from which we infer that Grant had contemplated a general advance on our lines with his whole force massed at Petersburg. If this is correct he got badly worsted. His strategy was a complete fizzle. The news from Petersburg which has just come in says we captured nine hundred prisoners, thirteen stands of colors, killed about seven hundred and have the same line as before.

Same Camp, August 2d. My Darling Nannie; We are camped in a sweet grove by the side of a large brick house, and I often wish you and your mother were here to enjoy it. I would like you to see Drewry's Bluff and the big cannon down there—big enough for you almost to crawl into. The breastworks there are very high and they have little rooms in them in which the powder and shells and shot are kept so they may not be injured either by rain or the shells of the enemy. The fortifications are all turfed which makes them look much nicer than any you have ever seen. The soldiers live in small cabins, all of which are whitewashed, and they have beautiful walkways between them and flowers and grass to make them look better. Would you like such soldiering as that? The fort is so situated that we could sink any yankee gunboats with our big guns if they try to pass up the James River, which is just at the foot of the bluff, to Richmond. We are camped at a place where there was a battle fought three months ago, and there are some very curious signs now left. Very near us the Yankees had their field hospital, and many of them are now buried all around us. In one hole they threw all the arms and legs they cut off, and as they threw only a little dirt over them many of them are sticking out now making a very horrid sight, but one we get used to. All the trees around us are marked with cannon and musket balls. A shell from one of our batteries struck a large oak tree and went to the heart of it before it exploded, then one piece of the shell went up the heart of the tree and the other down. It split the tree, of course, but stuck fast and stands there now like a great wedge. I hope the owner of the place will let it stand as it is as a memento of the war, which will be very striking when you are an old woman.

The most remarkable thing I have seen is a cabin a few hundred yards from here where a dead Yankee is lying still unburied. He seems to have been wounded and carried into this cabin and laid on some straw on the floor. There he died, and had, as many bodies do, dried up, for the cabin was between the two lines and neither side could get to him to aid him or bury him. Right by his side lies the body of a great Newfoundland dog, which the negroes at the house in which we are camped say died of starvation rather than leave his dead master. Master and dog lie there together, strangers in a strange land, unburied and unwept, and perhaps, far away in the North, he has some little girl like you who is still hoping for her father's return and picturing the joy of having him back and romping with the faithful dog. War is a sad thing but if the poor man had stayed home and not come down here to desolate our homes and burn our houses he would have been with his little girl now. The negroes say they tried to get him to leave his master. They tempted him with food. Once he came out, ate something, but went back and afterwards they could not get him to leave his place or eat anything. So, there he died. Men are not so faithful as dogs.

The Last Days of the Confederate Cause

Edward Porter Alexander

> A native of Georgia and a West Point graduate, Brigadier
> General Edward Porter Alexander was an artillerist and engi-
> neer who witnessed all the great battles of the Eastern theater
> as well as the surrender of General Robert E. Lee at Appo-
> mattox Court House in Virginia. After Appomattox, Alexan-
> der found himself in dire need of money, friends, and some
> notion of a future, which he imagined might take place some-
> where in South America, fighting new civil wars on a differ-
> ent continent. This excerpt from General Porter's private
> memoir, *Fighting for the Confederacy,* begins on April 9,
> 1865, as Ulysses S. Grant lays down the terms of surrender to
> General Lee at Appomattox.

The terms of the surrender were drawn up by Gen. Grant
himself in a brief note rapidly written, & all the details
as afterward carried out seem to me a remarkable model of
practical simplicity. This is Gen. Grant's letter, which, being accepted by Gen. Lee in a brief note, then became the
contract of surrender:

> Appomattox Ct.H., Va., April 9th, 1865
> General R.E. Lee, Commanding C.S.A.
> General: In accordance with the substance of my letter to you
> of the 8th inst., I propose to receive the surrender of the Army of
> Northern Virginia on the following terms, to wit: Rolls of all the

Excerpted from the memoirs of Edward Porter Alexander as they appear in *Fighting for
the Confederacy*, edited by Gary W. Gallagher (Chapel Hill: University of North Carolina Press, 1989).

officers and men to be made in duplicate, one copy to be given to an officer to be designated by me, the other to be retained by such officer or officers as you may designate. The officers to give their individual paroles not to take up arms against the Government of the United States until properly [exchanged], and each company or regimental commander to sign a like parole for the men of their commands. The arms, artillery, and public property to be parked, and stacked, and turned over to the officers appointed by me to receive them. This will not embrace the side-arms of the officers, nor their private horses or baggage. This done, each officer and man will be allowed to return to his home, not to be disturbed by the United States authorities so long as they observe their paroles, and the laws in force where they may reside.

Very respectfully,

U.S. Grant, Lieutenant-General

I've always been particularly impressed with the last sentence, which in such few & simple & unobjectionable words, practically gave an amnesty to every surrendered soldier for all political offences. The subject had not been discussed, nor referred to in any way. Nor did there seem, at that time, any likelihood that there would ever be any vindictive desire to hang or punish our prominent men for treason. Nor would there have been had Mr. Lincoln lived. But after his death there came a time when even Gen. Lee's blood was specially thirsted for, and when this provision enabled Gen. Grant to protect him even against President [Andrew] Johnson & with him every paroled soldier in the South. For the terms given by Gen. Grant were followed in the surrender of all the other armies. Gen. Horace Porter has told me personally of President Johnson's insisting that "the hanging should begin," & of Gen. Grant's threatening to resign from the command of the army if the protection he had promised to the surrendered were violated in a single instance. . . .

McLean's Bad Luck

I had to ride into the village [of Appomattox] two or three times on some matters of detail, & on the first occasion of going to the house in which the surrender had taken place, & which was still the headquarters, I was surprised to meet

Maj. Wilmer McLean, whom I mentioned in my narrative of Bull Run. He had married an aunt of my wife's, and his house on Bull Run had been Gen. [Pierre] Beauregard's head quarters during the affair at Blackburn's Ford, July 18th, 1861—the very first collision between the hostile armies in Va., the action being fought upon his lands. I had been intimate with himself & his family as long as the army was in that vicinity, but I had not seen him now for over two years. Said I, "Why, hello, McLean! What are you doing here?" He answered, "By Heavens, Alexander, what are *you* doing here?" He then went on & told me that his place on Bull Run had been so ravaged & torn up by the constant passage of armies that it became impossible to live there; & he had at last sold out & moved to Appomattox C.H., near-ly 200 miles, as a secluded spot where he could hope never to see a soldier. And then he pointed out his wrecked fences & trampled fields, over which infantry, artillery, & cavalry had contended on the 9th, & the headquarters in his yard & house & asked what I thought of that for luck. It was cer-tainly a very remarkable coincidence. The first hostile shot I ever saw strike, went through his kitchen. The last gun was fired on his land and the surrender took place in his parlor; nearly four years of time & 200 miles of space intervening.

A Touching Gesture

Of course I met at the Federal headquarters many old army friends & acquaintances & the courtesy, consideration, & good will of every one of them was shown in every way possible. Indeed, Gen. Grant's spirit of kindness seemed to imbue his whole army down to the private soldiers & the teamsters one met upon the roads, who would turn out into the mud for any Confederate officer, & salute him with a better grace & courtesy, doubtless, than they sometimes showed to their own officers.

Among those whom I met was one of my class-mates named Warner from Pa. We had never been in the least inti-mate as cadets, running in different circles entirely, & I doubt whether in the four years either of us was ever in the other's room. But Warner called me to one side, & said:

> Aleck, I guess you fellows haven't much money about you but
> Confederate, just now, & in your present situation it may be a lit-
> tle inconvenient. And you know our pay has been raised & we
> have just got greenbacks to burn. And I've just drawn several
> months' pay & I will really be very much obliged to you if you
> will let me lend you two or three hundred dollars, that you may
> return, if you insist upon it, sometime in the future, but if never it
> would be only the more grateful to me.

That touched me very deeply, coming from one to whom
I had really no special relations at all; but it is only a fair
sample of the spirit that breathed everywhere, & which I believe would have animated the North every where but for the
assassination of Lincoln.

Defeated and Insolent

*Defeat did not mean abject surrender for the people of the
South, who fearlessly expressed defiance of and hatred for the
Yankees, especially for Yankee officers occupying the Southern states of the former Confederacy. Bitter feelings toward
the North would continue through the period of Reconstruction and for decades afterward, as celebrated in a certain folk
song quoted by Gary Gallagher in* The Confederate War.

Northern soldiers frequently commented about the inso-
lence and animosity they perceived among former Confederates. One such observer was Union sergeant Mathew
Woodruff, who betrayed reciprocal dislike for white southerners in relating an incident in Mobile, Alabama. When a
black woman reprimanded three young girls for waving a
rebel flag, the children's mother "appeared with a saucy re-
buke & insults to all *Yanks,* saying 'they' (the South was not
whiped) & if they got a chance would rise again." Woodruff
believed these "to be the prevailing sentiments throughout
the South." He added, "There is not 9 out of 10 of these so

I did not accept Warner's generous offer, however, because I had just borrowed $200 in gold from Maj. W.H. Gibbes. He had been great friends of a Mr. Cameron of Petersburg, in whose house he lay while recovering from his severe wound received at the [Battle of the] Mine [near Petersburg, July 1864]. Cameron was a British subject & was largely interested in blockade-running & he gave Gibbes a chance to send out a bale of cotton, the profit on which was about $400 gold, & Gibbes had recently received it.

I was making all my preparations for Brazil. The Haskells were going to ride home to Abbeville, S.C., from Appomattox, & it would have been very nice to go with them & then on to Washington, Georgia. I have regretted a thousand times since that I did not. But I feared that if I once got down to Georgia I could not get off from there, either to go to Brazil,

---

called 'Whiped' traitors that I would trust until I saw the rope applied to their Necks, then I would only have Faith in the quality of the rope."

Sergeant Woodruff would have said that the song "O, I'm a Good Old Rebel"—the 1866 sheet music for which was sarcastically dedicated to "the Hon. Thad. Stevens"—accurately reflected widespread feelings among ex-Confederates. Its bitter lyrics combined pride in the Confederacy, recognition that further armed resistance was impossible, and determination to keep alive hatred for the Northern foe:

> Three hundred thousand Yankees is stiff in Southern dust.
> We got three hundred thousand before they conquered us.
> They died of Southern fever and Southern steel and shot,
> I wish they was three million instead of what we got.
>
> I can't take up my musket and fight them now no more,
> But I ain't gonna love them, now that is certain sure.
> And I don't want no pardon for what I was and am.
> I won't be reconstructed, and I don't care a damn.

Gary W. Gallagher, *The Confederate War.* Cambridge, MA: Harvard University Press, 1997.

or to find out anything about it. So I decided to go first from Appomattox C.H. to Washington City & [call] on the Brazilian minister. If he would send me to Brazil I would put myself in his hands. So I had borrowed $200.00 gold from Gibbes, & I had also gotten letters from Gen. Lee & Gen. Longstreet & Gen. [William] Pendleton, endorsing me as a good artillerist. So now, my men all paroled, my guns turned over to our captors, & money & letters in my pocket, I was ready to start.

Farewells

The Federals had opened the railroad from City Point on the James [River] via Petersburg to Burkeville, & I was invited to join a mixed party of Federals & Confederates who were to set out about 9 A.M. on the 12th for Burkeville. We spent the last night in the apple orchard and Wed. morning, Apr. 12th, marked the final breaking up & separation of my dearly beloved staff and the remnant of my battalion and of battery commanders.

I will not attempt to describe it. Just imagine yourself parting from your very dearest friends, after years of common danger & hardship; & now, in common disaster, saying farewell and separating apparently forever to face unknown futures. For I thought it possible that in a few weeks I might be actually fighting down in Paraguay.

Charley [Alexander's slave] was very anxious to accompany me; & would have gone anywhere on earth, but I gave him the ten dollars in gold which his accumulated hire had bought, as has already been told, & bade him good by, for it would have been impossible to take him.

The Haskells agreed to take along my horses, Dixie & Meg; & to send them over to Washington for me to my wife, & also to take a letter which I wrote telling her all about it. The mails had been very slow & I had had no letter from her now for over three weeks. To take me to Burkeville I had reserved a battery sergeant's horse which I would turn over at that place to the Federal quartermaster. And so at 9 A.M. on Wed., April 12th, I set out from Appomattox C.H. to seek my fortune again in the "wide, wide world."...

Dangerous Washington

Sunday evening [April 16] I first heard on the streets rumors of the assassination of Prest. Lincoln. I did not believe it & went to Gen. Ord's after supper to ask if it could be true. Gen. Ord confirmed it & advised me not to go to Washington City. But I did not know exactly what else I could do & decided to risk it. I left on Mon. morning in a boat which went down the James & up the Potomac, & landed me in Washn. on Tuesday the 18th.

I had no sooner landed than I felt it in the atmosphere that I was in the wrong place. The streets swarmed like beehives. The president's body was lying in the White House to be viewed, & the column, four deep, forming & marching past reached a half mile up Pa. Avenue.

Little was yet known of the plot which resulted in the murder, & it was naturally ascribed to Confederates in general. And somehow Mr. [Jefferson] Davis, Mr. [Henry] Clay, & others were supposed to be connected with it & rewards of $100,000 each were offered for their capture. The passion & excitement of the crowds were so great that anyone on the street, recognised merely as a Confederate, would have been instantly mobbed & lynched. In Richmond I had gotten a citizen coat & pants, & I wore a U.S. army private's overcoat, only dyed black instead of in its original blue. But, to a close observer, such a coat would seem particularly suspicious. However, being there I went to see the Brazilian minister. He read my letters & told me that if I should go to Brazil he had no doubt I could secure a commission in the Brazilian army, but he had no authority to speak on the matter or to send any one, nor any means to use to that end. Possibly, he said, the consul in N.Y. might render aid. He said that, I am sure, just to get rid of me. He seemed to be actually afraid lest my being in his house might bring a mob on him.

His suggestion of the consul in New York determined me to leave Washington on the train at 5 P.M. that afternoon. On the street I met my old friend Major—now Gen. Myer, chief signal officer. He was very cordial & took me to his house to lunch with Mrs. Myer. After leaving them I went to the office of Gen. Augur, commanding in the city, to get my pass made good to N.Y.

Augur's adjt. was Col. Jos. Taylor, one of my most special & intimate friends. As I walked up to his desk, he stared at me & said, "Great God! Alexander, what are you doing here?" "I am trying to get away," I said, "& I'll do it quick if you'll fix me these papers." "Well," said he, "old fellow, you had better. Yesterday a company of cavalry brought in your Confederate General Payne, who had surrendered up at Leesburg, & the crowd started after him to hang him. It was all the soldiers could do to stop them long enough for us to run Payne out the back way & put him in a hack & take him to the Old Capital Prison where we have him now, locked up for his own safety."

Cloak and Dagger

On looking at my papers Taylor decided to send me to Grant's office, which he did, with a soldier to conduct me; & there my pass was fixed by some subordinate & I saw no one whom I knew. Then I went by the old National Hotel for my hand baggage, left there in the morning, & took a street car to the B.&O. Railway station. I knew the city was swarming with detectives, amateur & regular, all stimulated by the enormous rewards offered for every one connected with the murder plot; and, as I got out of the street car, I spotted one of them standing on the side walk & evidently sizing up the people coming to take the train.

My dyed soldier's overcoat & my $500 Richmond boots, with my pants tucked inside, evidently took his eye, & he turned down the side walk so as to be abreast of me as I reached it. I tried to shake him, as if casually, by long quick strides across the muddy street; but he was also quick. So, on the side walk, I came down to a very leisurely gait to let him pass. But he also slowed down as he drew along side of me & said, "Good evening, Sir." "Good evening," said I with a blandness . . ."Going to Baltimore?" said he. "Yes," said I; & butter, in my mouth, would have thought itself in a refrigerator. "So am I," said he. "Ah?" said I, with an accent of utterly indifferent good nature, plainer than the nose on most people's faces. "Yes," said he, "seems to be a big crowd"—as we entered the big waiting room. I grunted a polite "Um Hoo," & we joined in the swarm of hundreds pressing into the funnel shaped space before the ticket seller's window. I was awfully scared. During all the war my favorite nightmare had been to dream of being in the Federal lines & in danger of arrest as a spy; & now, here was a situation very like it. But I continued to play my hand with a coolness & nonchalance that seemed to me really inspired. It was a pushing crowd & presently some man pushed to get between me & my friend. I *apparently* resisted but I let him in. And I played that game so carefully & so well that when we came near the neck of the funnel he was some three or four files ahead of me. But I heard him say, "Ticket to Baltimore," & the agent answered, "This is [the] New York train. No Baltimore tickets sold until this train has gone. Pass on please." He motioned to me & tried to speak, but I was looking another way & he was squeezed along. As my turn came I had my money ready & said "N.Y." in a low tone, got my ticket, & shot through the train gate a little ways ahead, & hid myself in the most distant & darkest corner I could find in a long train of about a dozen coaches. I saw my friend no more, the train starting in a short while. . . .

In Savannah

On Saturday morning, April 29th, I started in the buggy with Col. [Lauton] Singleton, but our progress was very brief. At the edge of the town the road ran between the high Central Railroad embankment on one side, & a fence on the other. A dead mule lay at the foot of the embankment. Our animal took fright at it, & whirled around, breaking our shafts to splinters. I could have cried with vexation. We could not get another buggy until the next day. I was hampered somewhat by being a guest in the matter & could not drive & push & kick as I might otherwise have done, if it had been a matter of business only. So on Sunday the 30th we made a fresh start. The roads were heavy with sand & we only accomplished 36 miles, putting up for the night at "Uncle Billy Moore's," a very nice country place where they took in travellers.

The next day we reached Col. Singleton's to dinner, 18 miles. His wife was a remarkably pretty & accomplished young woman, with a lot of children too; & their hospitality would by no means let me press on in the afternoon as I wished. Even the next day they were reluctant to let me go; but at last took me on about 18 miles more, to a Mr. Jno. M. Miller's, who could get me into Waynesboro in time for the train on Wednesday by an early start. That landed me in Augusta Wednesday night. And on Thursday morning, May 4th, I took the train for Washington [Georgia], & arrived, at last, about noon.

But I heard on the train that I was too late to see Mr. Davis. He had arrived with his party in Washington at 10 A.M. the day before. Some of his cabinet were already there, & others came with him. The last cabinet meeting had been held in the afternoon in the old bank building of which my father had been cashier during my youth. At that meeting he parted with his cabinet & elected to become a fugitive. He left the town that night, May 3rd, at ten o'clock, with a single attendant; & followed his family, who had arrived on Apr. 30th & left on May 1st. He was captured with them near Irwinville on the morning of May 10th. I have always believed, and I believe today, that if I could have seen him in Washington he would have elected to surrender himself. I had later news of the situation at the North than any one else, & I had, by chance, Gen. Lee's expressed opinion as to the only proper & dignified course for himself, which would apply with more force to President Davis. It has always been & always will be one of the disappointments of my life that I was too late to see him. It *might* have changed for the better many subsequent events.

But the dead mule was lying on the Central Railroad embankment at Savannah.

With a darkey carrying my valise, stuffed with my New York Mills & pongee [imitation silk] & other purchases at Stewarts, I started from the railroad depot, where I had landed, for my father's house. Nearly the whole family was now collected there by the military & political events which happened for a while to center upon the town. The Haskells had sent over my horse & my letter from Appomattox, telling of my plans, & I was supposed by all to be en route to Brazil.

Passing through the public square, I accidentally met Gen. Lawton, the first one from whom I could learn any personal news. He turned & walked with me home telling me of all that had happened. I had a little daughter born on April 7th & my wife was still very weak & ill.

But although she thought me far on my road to Brazil, she knew the rush of my feet up the stairs the moment that she heard it, & as I opened the door she was in the middle of the room advancing to meet me.

Chronology

1860
December 20: The legislature of South Carolina proclaims that the union between the state and the United States of America is formally dissolved.

1861
January 9–February 1: Alabama, Florida, Georgia, Louisiana, Mississippi, and Texas secede from the Union.

February 8: Southern politicians establish the Confederate States of America and elect Jefferson Davis as the Confederate president at a convention in Montgomery, Alabama.

March 4: Abraham Lincoln is inaugurated as president of the United States.

April 12: Shore batteries belonging to South Carolina's militia open fire on Fort Sumter, a U.S. installation in Charleston harbor.

April 17: A Virginia convention passes an ordinance of secession; eight days later Virginia joins the Confederate States of America.

May 21: The Confederate government moves its capital to Richmond, Virginia.

July 21: Southern forces win the first major victory of the Civil War at the Battle of First Manassas, or Bull Run.

1862
February 13: Fort Donelson, Tennessee, falls to Union forces under Ulysses S. Grant.

March 9: Two ironclad ships, the *Monitor* and the *Merrimack,* fight to a standoff at Hampton Roads, Virginia.

April 6: Confederate and Union forces clash at the Battle of Shiloh; the Union comes away with a costly victory.

April 16: The Confederate government passes the first national conscription act, drafting all able-bodied, nonexempt men between eighteen and thirty-five for three years' service.

April 25: New Orleans, Louisiana, the South's busiest commercial port, is captured by a Union fleet and is occupied by Union forces under General Benjamin Butler.

May 31: The Confederate army battles Union forces to a draw at the Battle of Fair Oaks, Virginia; after the battle, President Jefferson Davis appoints General Robert E. Lee commander of the Army of Northern Virginia.

June 6: Memphis, Tennessee, falls to Union forces.

August 29–30: Generals Lee and Thomas "Stonewall" Jackson lead the Confederates to victory at the Battle of Second Manassas.

September 17: The Battle of Sharpsburg, or Antietam, takes place in western Maryland, stopping a Confederate drive on Washington.

September 22: President Lincoln delivers a preliminary Emancipation Proclamation, formally freeing the slaves of the Confederacy as of January 1, 1863.

October 8: A Confederate invasion of Kentucky is stopped by the Union army at the Battle of Perryville.

December 13: Union forces suffer a resounding defeat at Fredericksburg, Virginia.

1863

January 1: President Lincoln issues the formal Emancipation Proclamation.

March 4: The Confederate armies defeat the Union at the Battle of Chancellorsville; Stonewall Jackson later dies of wounds received during the battle.

April 24: The Confederate government passes a new income tax law as well as a 10-percent levy of all food produced on Confederate farms.

June 30–July 2: The Army of Northern Virginia is defeated at the Battle of Gettysburg.

July 4: The fortress of Vicksburg, Mississippi, falls after a long siege, allowing the Union to control the entire Mississippi River valley.

September 20: The Confederate army under General Braxton Bragg wins the Battle of Chickamauga.

November 25: Confederate forces are defeated in the Battle of Chattanooga.

1864

May 5: A long campaign through Virginia begins with the Battle of the Wilderness.

June 3: The Union army under General Grant is stopped at the Battle of Cold Harbor.

June 20: The Union begins a siege of Petersburg, Virginia.

July 11–12: General Jubal Early leads a daring Confederate cavalry raid into the outskirts of Washington, D.C., but is thrown back.

September 2: Union general William Sherman captures Atlanta.

November 8: President Lincoln is reelected, vowing to carry the war through to complete Union victory.

November 15: Sherman begins a devastating "march to the sea" between Atlanta and Savannah, Georgia, destroying everything in his path.

1865

February 3: A peace conference is convened at Hampton Roads, Virginia, but Union and Confederate negotiators fail to reach an agreement.

February 6: Davis appoints General Lee commander in chief of the Confederate army.

April 2: The Confederate army abandons Richmond.

April 9: General Lee surrenders to General Grant at Appomattox Courthouse, Virginia.

April 14: President Lincoln is assassinated in Washington, D.C.

April 26: Confederate general Joe Johnston surrenders to Union general William T. Sherman at Raleigh, North Carolina.

May 26: The last Confederate troops surrender.

For Further Research

E.P. Alexander, *Military Memoirs of a Confederate*. Bloomington: Indiana University Press, 1962.

Eliza Frances Andrews, *The War-Time Journal of a Georgia Girl*. Atlanta: Cherokee, 1976.

John Bakeless, *Spies of the Confederacy*. Mineola, NY: Dover, 1997.

Carleton Beals, *War Within a War: The Confederacy Against Itself*. Philadelphia: Chilton Books, 1965.

Robert C. Black III, *The Railroads of the Confederacy*. Chapel Hill: University of North Carolina Press, 1998.

Heros von Borcke, *Memoirs of the Confederate War for Independence*. New York: Peter Smith, 1938.

John Bowers, *Chickamauga and Chattanooga: The Battles That Doomed the Confederacy*. New York: HarperCollins, 1994.

Edward Boykin, *Ghost Ship of the Confederacy: The Story of the "Alabama" and Her Captain, Raphael Semmes*. New York: Funk & Wagnalls, 1957.

Hamilton Cochran, *Blockade Runners of the Confederacy*. Indianapolis: Bobbs-Merrill, 1958.

John Esten Cooke, *Wearing of the Gray*. Bloomington: Indiana University Press, 1959.

Thomas W. Cutrer and T. Michael Parrish, eds., *Brothers in Gray: The Civil War Letters of the Pierson Family*. Baton Rouge: Louisiana State University Press, 1997.

Burke Davis, *The Long Surrender*. New York: Random House, 1985.

William C. Davis, *The Cause Lost: Myths and Realities of the Confederacy*. Lawrence: University Press of Kansas, 1996.

————, *"A Government of Our Own": The Making of the Confederacy.* New York: Free, 1994.

————, *The Orphan Brigade: The Kentucky Confederates Who Couldn't Go Home.* Garden City, NY: Doubleday, 1980.

Henry Kyd Douglas, *I Rode with Stonewall.* Chapel Hill: University of North Carolina Press, 1940.

Clifford Dowdey, *Death of a Nation: The Story of Lee and His Men at Gettysburg.* New York: Alfred A. Knopf, 1958.

Charles East, ed., *Sarah Morgan: The Civil War Diary of a Southern Woman.* New York: Touchstone, 1991.

Drew Gilpin Faust, *Mothers of Invention: Women of the Slaveholding South in the American Civil War.* Chapel Hill: University of North Carolina Press, 1996.

Douglas Southall Freeman, *Lee's Lieutenants: A Study in Command.* New York: Charles Scribner's Sons, 1942.

Gary W. Gallagher, *The Confederate War: How Popular Will, Nationalism, and Military Strategy Could Not Stave Off Defeat.* Cambridge, MA: Harvard University Press, 1997.

————, ed., *Fighting for the Confederacy: The Personal Recollections of General Edward Porter Alexander.* Chapel Hill: University of North Carolina Press, 1989.

Mark Grimsley, *The Hard Hand of War: Union Military Policy Towards Southern Civilians, 1861–1865.* New York: Cambridge University Press, 1995.

Parthenia Antoinette Hague, *A Blockaded Family: Life in Southern Alabama During the Civil War.* Boston: Houghton, Mifflin, 1888.

Henry E. Handerson, *Yankee in Gray: The Civil War Memoirs of Henry E. Handerson.* Cleveland, OH: Press of Western Reserve University, 1962.

Tony Horwitz, *Confederates in the Attic: Dispatches from the Unfinished Civil War.* New York: Pantheon Books, 1998.

John B. Jones, *A Rebel War Clerk's Diary.* New York: Sagamore, 1958.

Mills Lane, ed., *"Dear Mother: Don't Grieve About Me. If I Get Killed, I'll Only Be Dead."* Savannah, GA: Beehive, 1977.

Elizabeth D. Leonard, *All the Daring of the Soldiers: Women of the Civil War Armies.* New York: W.W. Norton, 1999.

Cornelia Peake McDonald, *A Woman's Civil War: A Diary, with Reminiscences of the War, from March 1862.* Madison: University of Wisconsin Press, 1992.

James M. McPherson, *For Cause and Comrades: Why Men Fought in the Civil War.* New York: Oxford University Press, 1997.

Jim Murphy, *The Boys' War: Confederate and Union Soldiers Talk About the Civil War.* New York: Clarion Books, 1990.

William C. Oates, *The War Between the Union and the Confederacy.* New York: Neale, 1905.

William G. Stevenson, *Thirteen Months in the Rebel Army.* New York: A.S. Barnes, 1959.

Robert Stiles, *Four Years Under Marse Robert.* New York: Neale, 1910.

Peter Svenson, *Battlefield: Farming a Civil War Battleground.* Winchester, MA: Faber and Faber, 1992.

Ben Ames Williams, ed., *A Diary from Dixie by Mary Boykin Chesnut.* Cambridge, MA: Harvard University Press, 1980.

Steven E. Woodworth, *Davis and Lee at War.* Lawrence: University Press of Kansas, 1998.

Index